Praise for *Gather God's People*

Gather God's People is a manual for corporate worship filled with wisdom, practicality, and biblical rooting. Whether or not one holds to the exact form or philosophy of worship put forth in this book, every reader will find great stimulation and strong biblical support for each of the various aspects of the theology and practice of worship advanced. Few books discuss with such clarity the range of issues and practices this book takes up, and it does so in an engaging and winsome manner. As pastors and worship leaders take to heart insights from this book, local churches and their worship services will surely be blessed.

Bruce A. Ware, professor of Christian theology at The Southern Baptist Theological Seminary

What an exceptionally helpful book! As a pastor and church planter with a generationally diverse congregation, I found this book to be a fantastic resource for helping us think through what we do when we gather. Brian and Jason have cut through the polarizing chatter on the topic of worship to provide a helpful framework for crafting our corporate gathering. More than just presenting concepts, they take us with them into their own planning sessions. Whether you are on staff at a large congregation or a volunteer in the band at a new church plant, this book will serve you well. It needs to be in the hands of anyone participating in your worship gathering.

Matthew Spandler-Davison, pastor of Redeemer Fellowship Church, Bardstown, Kentucky, and executive director of 20schemes.com

Christian worship must be built upon, shaped by, and saturated with the word of God. In this helpful book, Croft and Adkins challenge us to think biblically through every aspect of corporate worship. From theological foundations to practical help, this book will help equip you in leading God's people.

Matt Boswell, pastor of ministries and worship, Providence Church, Frisco, Texas, and Founder of Doxology & Theology

This is the book on planning corporate worship which I've been looking for! Drawing from years of local church ministry, rooted in sound theology, and written with pastoral care this book is a wonderfully helpful resource for all those involved in planning corporate worship services. Croft and Adkins engage worship planning with intentionality, carefulness and joy, writing with theological conviction as well as awareness of differences among God's people and awareness of particular needs and situations of each local congregation. I also particularly appreciate their encouragement for churches to re-engage the historic practice of singing the psalms. I heartily commend this book!

Ray Van Neste, PhD, professor of biblical studies at Union University

GATHER GOD'S PEOPLE

Understand, Plan, and Lead Worship in Your Local Church

BRIAN CROFT
AND JASON ADKINS

ZONDERVAN®

ZONDERVAN

Gather God's People

This title is also available as a Zondervan ebook.
Visit www.zondervan.com/ebooks.

Requests for information should be addressed to:

Zondervan, *3900 Sparks Dr. SE, Grand Rapids, Michigan 49546*

Library of Congress Cataloging-in-Publication Data

Croft, Brian.
Gather God's people : understand, plan, and lead worship in your local church / Brian Croft and Jason Adkins.
p. cm. (Practical shepherding series)
ISBN 978-0-310-51935-5
1. Public worship. I. Adkins, Jason. II. Title
BV15.C76 2015
264–dc23 2014022269

Cover design and illustrations: Jay Smith—Juicebox Designs
Interior design: Matthew Van Zomeren

Printed in the United States of America

HB 04.11.2024

To Greg Van Court,
a beloved and faithful fellow laborer—
we fondly remember how you nourished us
with prayer and the reading of God's word

CONTENTS

PART 3: LEAD WORSHIP

FOREWORD

DETERMINING WHAT THE CHURCH should do when we gather on Sundays has contributed to no small number of tense discussions, heated debates, and church splits throughout the centuries. Christians rightly want to know what pleases God when we meet. After all, Paul admonishes us, "Do not be foolish, but understand what the Lord's will is" (Ephesians 5:17). That includes our corporate gatherings.

But even when we agree that Scripture is our only authority, church meetings can end up looking vastly different from each other. That's due to a number of factors. Some leaders are influenced by a business marketing model. They define success by communication skills, administrative excellence, and numerical growth. Others focus on facilitating meaningful personal encounters with God. They value individual emotional engagement and provide a buffet line of options for worshipers to choose from that might include painting, lighting candles, or reflecting on images. Still others emphasize the importance of tradition. Their meetings include a variety of elements, mostly chosen for how they connect people to practices and prayers proven over centuries.

Brian Croft and Jason Adkins offer a different approach. They really believe God's word is sufficient to guide us when it comes to matters related to the church meeting on Sundays. While God hasn't told us everything we'd like to know about what to do when we meet, he has communicated clearly what we need to know. We don't have to scour the Internet to find elements that are more interesting, approaches that are more innovative, or content that is more relevant. What matters most is right in front of us in the pages of our Bibles.

As I read through this book I was grateful for the wisdom that has come from years of study and experience. It's right in line with what I've come to know of Brian through our friendship over the past ten years. Brian and Jason haven't written mere theory. They share abundant examples of ways they've fleshed out their biblical convictions. But their goal isn't to persuade us that our churches should look exactly like theirs. Rather, they want us to ask hard questions about whether we've thought biblically about corporate worship (hint: it's more than music), and whether our beliefs have led to more intentional preparation resulting in more fruitful leadership.

While any leader will benefit from reading this book, not every leader will benefit in the same way. You may realize you need to hammer out the details of your theology of worship. You may discover tools and practices that will help you in your planning. Or you may be equipped to pray publicly, read Scripture, lead singing, and administer baptism and the Lord's Supper in ways that are more Christ exalting.

A common problem among leaders is thinking that God can't use us because we lack certain gifts. You may not have the most charismatic personality. You may not have thousands of people downloading your sermons or subscribing to a weekly podcast; you may not even have a podcast. You may consider your administrative and technological skills to be just average.

That's okay. Wherever you're at and whatever kind of church you lead, this book will remind you of the great things God can accomplish through any leader who submits joyfully and faithfully to his word in the power of his Spirit.

Understanding, planning, and leading congregational worship is the responsibility and privilege of every pastor. I have no doubt that what's written in the following pages can help you do it more effectively and enable you to enjoy Sunday meetings that are more thoughtful, emotionally engaging, and life transforming.

Bob Kauflin, Sovereign Grace Church of Louisville, Kentucky, and director of Sovereign Grace Music

ACKNOWLEDGMENTS

BRIAN AND JASON WOULD LIKE TO THANK . . .

Zondervan, for your commitment to this Practical Shepherding series and for giving a platform for the needed conversations this book will start.

Anthony Luppino and Mike Mackison, former pastoral interns, who, after sitting in on our weekly service planning meetings, strongly insisted this book be written.

Adam Embry, for helping us think through the craft of service planning and supporting the practice of psalm singing.

Auburndale Baptist Church, for bearing with us as we have learned together to "worship by the book."

Our wives, pleasant vines (Psalm 128) who give joy and strength to all of our endeavors.

Our great God and Father of our Lord Jesus Christ, who is so worthy to be worshiped thoughtfully and intentionally when his redeemed people gather together.

INTRODUCTION

I (BRIAN) HAVE A CONFESSION TO MAKE. Jason, my coauthor, is really the one who wrote this book. His gifts to think clearly and creatively craft an argument are evident throughout its pages. He has a unique writing voice that is quite different from mine, but it's a voice that will serve you well. Since this book primarily reflects the diligent writing labors of Jason, you may be asking, "Why the coauthorship?" Well, to be fair, there are a few places where I directly contribute in the writing, but the main reason for our dual authorship is the origin of these ideas. Jason captured the content of this book, but much of it reflects my convictions and experiences over two decades of planning and leading God's people in corporate worship.

My experiences are diverse. I have planned and led worship services in a small rural church where the hymnal was as sacred as the Bible. I have crafted and led services where thousands of teenagers have gathered to be energized and moved, and to meet with God. I have served on a music staff of a church that weekly planned and led services seeking to blend all kinds of different styles and preferences in a large church setting. For those who don't know what that looks like, imagine being the one to lead a hymn and then cue the smoke machine later in the same service. (Yes, I did. Could I make something like that up?) And that was just the first decade. When I put behind me these experiences to become the senior pastor of a small struggling Southern Baptist church, you'd think I would have faced a significant identity crisis. And yet, it was quite the opposite.

My wide range of experiences in planning and leading corporate worship in all these different venues firmly solidified what would become deep convictions in my soul about what truly glorifies God in the public gathering of his people and what does not. Does the Bible give any guidance on these matters, or is it simply about preferences? Are there methods that help facilitate what God desires? Are there more effective ways to lead that either encourage participation or stifle it? Ultimately, what should the public gathering of the local church be about? Every church I served would have answered these questions differently. In God's kind and providential design of my journey, he used that diversity to help drive me to his word to find the answers.

The content of this book and the ideas herein reflect my answers to those questions. They represent how I shepherd and lead my church in matters of public worship. I believe God does inform us on how he desires to be worshiped. And God has given direction on what elements are to be present when the church gathers. God desires a certain *kind* of participation from his people.

Jason entered this journey with me five years ago when he came on staff at our church, and he has brought a fresh perspective and several new ideas to the work I was trying to cultivate in our church. He helped take my intentionality and my efforts to be faithful to a whole new level. For that I am grateful, and because of this shared work, Jason was the perfect partner in both the development and writing of all you will find in these pages. He has captured the essence of my convictions and practices from the last decade with a precision and clarity I fear I would have lacked if I had undertaken to organize and write them alone.

As Jason will remind you throughout this book, our convictions have shaped the implementation of this book's concepts at our church in a way that may be different from yours. We suggest these ideas in love and charity, knowing there are many different faithful churches in different contexts that need to approach things differently. We write them simply as an example of one church seeking to be faithful to God and his word in our context and in the way he prescribes to be worshiped. Be challenged where we differ. Be affirmed where we are unified. Most of all, allow this book to aid you in your biblical understanding of corporate worship, in how to best plan for it, and in how to effectively and faithfully conduct it so that God alone is passionately praised by his redeemed people.

Introduction

PART 1

UNDERSTAND WORSHIP

CHAPTER 1

BIBLICAL THEOLOGY OF WORSHIP

MINISTERS WHO DESIRE TO LEAD their congregations in God-honoring worship must lead with an understanding of the Bible's teaching on worship. A failure of theological leadership will leave God's people unanchored, carried about by every wind of human cunning (Ephesians 4:14). In matters of Christian worship, ministers who do not lead theologically hand over the role of leadership to passing cultural fads or venerated traditions. Our criticism of superficial, romanticized modern worship music, on the one hand, and of saccharin, sentimental classics, on the other hand, is shallow if we do not teach God's people the Bible's message about worship.

Within the pages of the Old and New Testaments, God has graciously met our need for a theological vision for worship. Through the Old Testament, Christians learn that God cares deeply how he is worshiped. In the New Testament, God explicitly teaches believers how he is to be worshiped. These two theological premises protect believers from worldly craftiness dictating the pace of Christian worship.

Worship in the Old Testament

A reiterated theme of the Old Testament is God's regard for himself. He is committed steadfastly to his glory and honor and seeks to make himself known through the key Old Testament events of creation, exodus, exile, and the promise of a new covenant. God's devotion to the glory of his name provides a foundation for other Old Testament phenomena, including worship regulations in the law, penalties for violating these regulations, and the frequent commands for God's people to praise him.

The primary function of the created order is to testify to the creative excellence and skill of God. He designed creation to reveal his character and unveil specific attributes. As humans perceive the beauty of the dawn, dusk, and night sky, they perceive a visual witness of "the glory of God" (Psalm 19:1) and a declaration of the great Judge's "righteousness" (Psalm 50:6).

God's dealings with his people, the Israelites, also reflect his desire for glory. He created his covenant people and called them by his name for his own glory (Isaiah 43:7). His plan for this people, which he revealed to Abraham, involved bondage in and deliverance from Egypt (Genesis 15:12–16). The purpose of the extraordinary events of the exodus is to show the Egyptians the exclusive dominance of the God of Israel (Exodus 7:15; 8:10, 22; 9:14, 29–30; 10:2; 14:4, 18).

Events throughout Old Testament history remind readers of God's intention of glorifying himself. Through extraordinary circumstances, the people of Israel enter the land God promised them. God causes the Jordan River to part, and the people cross the river on dry land. The purpose of this impressive display was that "all the peoples of the earth might know that the hand of the LORD is powerful" (Joshua 4:24). Furthermore, God orchestrates Israel's conquest and occupancy of the land in such a way that precludes Israel's boasting and credits him duly for Israel's victories (Joshua 6:16; Judges 7:2).

This theme—God's intent to glorify himself—persists even as Israel rejects God. God grants wicked King Ahab a victory over Syria in order to reiterate to Ahab God's character (1 Kings 20:13). For that same reason, the prophet Elijah confronted Ahab's false prophets (1 Kings 18:36). However, Israel continues to rebel, and God brings about the curses of the law and sends his people away from the land promised to them. Israel's exile and eventual return from exile share a common purpose. God exiles Israel because he "had concern" for his holy name (Ezekiel 36:21), and he extends mercy to exiled Israel for the sake of his holy name (Ezekiel 36:22).

God's regard for himself and his desire for his own glory are traits that sometimes confuse believers. Any human with this kind of self-regard would face charges of narcissism. Yet, what makes the human pursuit of glory vapid is each human's inherent imperfections. Not a single one of us deserves glory. God, however, in his exemplary holiness, radiant beauty, inscrutable wisdom, and scores of other perfect virtues, is worthy of all adulation, affection, and acceptance, and because he is omniscient, he knows his worthiness. Would we not think less of God if he thought less of himself?

Understanding God's regard for himself and his glory clarifies the worship practices of the Old Testament. The phenomena of Old Testament worship orbit around the weighty truth of God's concern for his glory. The extensive worship regulations, for instance, find their ground and legitimation in God's desire for his own glory. Moses devotes six chapters of the book of Exodus (chapters 25–30) to the Lord's instructions regarding the design of a place for his worship. He later uses five chapters (chapters 36–40) to describe how Israelite craftsmen follow these instructions. This attention to detail communicates God's desire for his glory. He cares deeply about how he is worshiped.

God's commitment to his glory explains the severity of punishment that God levies against those who violate worship regulations. Aaron's sons, Nadab and Abihu, conducted priestly worship outside of God's guidelines. They provided an offering that was contrary to God's command (Leviticus 10:1). Tragically, Nadab and Abihu die "before the LORD" because of this sin (verse 2). God earnestly seeks the worship of his name, but he wills this worship to conform to his standards. The severity of this particular judgment communicates the extent to which God cares about his glory in worship.

The prevalence of calls to worship in the Old Testament makes sense in light of God's passion for his fame. Particularly in the book of Psalms, God frequently commands his people, and even all peoples, to praise him. Over thirty times, we receive the command, "Praise the LORD," and the psalmists use many other imperatives, including "Ascribe to the LORD ..." (Psalm 29:2), "let us bow down in worship" (95:6), and "Sing to the LORD" (149:1). With these entreaties, God is not fishing for compliments, lacking confidence, or seeking assurance. These commands are decrees from a Judge who preserves justice. One being in all the universe deserves all glory and all praise; therefore, "Praise the LORD!"

In the way God has created the world, treated his people, commanded his praise, intricately specified worship practices, and judged the disobedient, he has sought his fame, glory, and honor. The Old Testament, then, reveals to us God, who cares deeply for how he is worshiped.

Worship in the New Testament

The God who deeply cares how he is worshiped—as revealed in the Old Testament—is the God who takes great care to teach Christians how to worship in the New Testament. The nature of Christian worship, as well as the activities of Christian worship, are explicitly set forth in the gospels and in the epistles of Paul.

Christian worship is spiritual and truthful. As Jesus dialogues with a sinful Samaritan woman, their views on worship begin to contrast with one another. She is preoccupied with matters of genealogy and geography. The right lineage ("our father Jacob," John 4:12) and locale ("our ancestors worshiped on this mountain," John 4:20) are the criteria she emphasizes for right worship. However, Jesus contests these notions and twice points to "spirit" and "truth" as the standards for God-honoring worship (John 4:23–24 ESV). Worshiping in "spirit" implies that proper praise involves the affections, the emotions, the desires, and the will. No longer does worship primarily revolve around physical acts, such as animal sacrifices. Worshiping in "truth" centralizes praise in Jesus Christ. He is the one who provides access to God the Father (Ephesians 2:18).

Apart from Jesus Christ—and the truthful good news about his deity, incarnation, death, resurrection, and second coming—worship lacks credibility and truthfulness.

Christian worship is purposeful. The apostle Paul operates from this principle as he instructs the church at Corinth about worship. In corporate worship, Paul in his own practice sought to sing with his mind (his understanding) and his spirit (1 Corinthians 14:15). This means Christian worship is not a freewheeling experience that concerns itself only with emotive, spontaneous responses. Christian worship is equally an intellectual enterprise—one in which believers acknowledge, confess, and profess propositional truth. By engaging the mind and the spirit in worship, Christians edify one another and testify to the truth before unbelievers. By purposefully addressing mind and spirit, Christians imitate God, who is not a "God of disorder" (1 Corinthians 14:33), and they do all things "in a fitting and orderly way" (verse 40).

Christian worship is congregational. The New Testament in pattern and precept defines worship in the context of the local church. The early post-Pentecost church gathered frequently to receive teaching, participate in the Lord's Supper, and pray (Acts 2:42). Though the number of believers in Jerusalem was significant (three thousand, according to Acts 2:41), the congregation still gathered in unison, though doing so required a large public venue (Solomon's Colonnade, Acts 5:12). New Testament commands for worship often imply the participation of the entire local congregation. For instance, the commands to sing to one another (Ephesians 5:18–21; Colossians 3:15–16) involve the whole congregation in encouraging one another.

The New Testament often includes commands that indicate what God expects to occur in Christian worship. An expectation for all Christians is to regularly gather for worship (Hebrews 10:25). These gatherings are the context for gospel ministers to fulfill their charge of preaching God's word (Acts 6:4; 2 Timothy 4:1–2). The New Testament depicts and expects churches to have an active corporate prayer life, which includes supplications for other believers (James 5:14), ministers (Colossians 4:3), and civil authorities (1 Timothy 2:1–2). Churches are commanded to sing when they gather (Ephesians 5:18–21; Colossians 3:15–16). The reading of God's word is a command repeated in the New Testament (Colossians 4:16; 1 Timothy 4:13). The ordinances of baptism and the Lord's Supper form an important part of the church's gathering, with the former constituting the mission of the church (Matthew 28:19–20) and the latter enduring until Christ's return (1 Corinthians 11:26). All of these commands ought to inform and shape the worship practices of local churches. God has carefully taught believers how to worship when they gather together.

Applying a Biblical Theology of Worship

A summary of the Old Testament's teaching on worship is that God cares deeply how he is worshiped, and a summary of the New Testament's teaching on worship is that God has specifically instructed believers on how to worship him. Christian ministers must understand and apply these principles as they oversee their local congregations. These principles give church leaders the theological vision needed for planning and leading worship.

These two summary statements cohere well with one another. If God cares deeply how he is worshiped and if God has given us specific instructions on worshiping him, then Christians ought to prioritize these commands in their worship. When churches gather, the preaching and reading of God's word, corporate prayer, congregational singing, and practice of the ordinances are essential. These practices are the means God has devised and ordained for glorifying himself in the local church. The right use of these means in the church's worship strengthens believers. Furthermore, intentional, orderly worship best communicates the gospel to unbelievers who have gathered with the congregation (1 Corinthians 14:23–26).

A wise way for applying these biblical principles and prioritizing these commands is what has often been called the regulative principle. God's word gives us precise parameters for worship. The New Testament, in particular, regulates worship. What it commands Christians to do in their gatherings ought to be the substance and sum of congregational worship. Whatever else creative Christians propose for worship lacks warrant in God's word. Though these proposals may have benefit in certain contexts, they are out of place in worship gatherings of the church. God is eager for his glory; he would not leave any essentials for the worship of his name unrevealed.

The following chapters guide ministers in understanding and applying the elements of Christian worship that are demanded by God's word. Much of the material provides practical guidance on planning and leading worship. However, before any of these suggestions are adopted by ministers and embraced by local churches, the theological concepts of God's devotion to his glory and his meticulous commands for worship must be affirmed. Pastors, love these doctrines from God's word and teach your congregation to love them also. Only in this doctrinally rich context will the application of these principles flourish.

CHAPTER 2

ELEMENTS OF WORSHIP

A HELPFUL ARTICULATION of the regulative principle, which has been offered by authors such as Mark Dever, Paul Alexander, and Ligon Duncan, is to preach the Bible, read the Bible, pray the Bible, sing the Bible, and see the Bible.[1] Describing Christian worship in this way allows God's authoritative and inspired word to shape the form and content of worship. In the following sections, we provide a biblical description of these elements, articulate the benefits of these elements, and give some suggestions on the format of these elements.

Preach the Word

God has ordained the preaching of his word as the essential means for conversion. This belief was so basic for the apostle Paul that he questioned how unbelievers would become Christians "without someone preaching" (Romans 10:14). God's word is useful for the full range of Christian ministry, including teaching, rebuking, correcting, and training (2 Timothy 3:16). Since God's word has this kind of usefulness, the Christian minister must "preach the word" (2 Timothy 4:2). The local church has always been the place for people who devote themselves to receiving the teaching of God's word (Acts 2:42).

Elements of Worship

The importance of preaching should have a foundational impact on the planning of worship. Local church leaders must not detract from the importance of preaching in attitude, deed, or word. Sometimes a pastor commends the worship accompanists with this kind of jest: "That music was so great; I think we could all go home after that." Another common attitude is to equate worship primarily with music, as though worship ends with the song before the sermon and resumes with the song after the sermon. However, because God's word is useful and because preaching unleashes the profitability of God's word, the preaching of God's word is truly the highlight of the local church's weekly gathering.

A practical way to portray the importance of preaching is to plan worship elements in a way that supports the sermon. In our worship planning, the Scripture readings, songs, and prayers all take their cue from the sermon. Those planning worship read the upcoming sermon texts throughout the week, along with sermon outlines. Worship planners can use keywords and central themes from sermon texts and outlines to identify songs and Scripture readings that cohere with the message of the sermon. All the service elements prepare the congregation to receive God's word with the intended result that the preached word will set the pace for the congregation's discipleship throughout the week.

A team approach is also helpful in worship planning. When the one who will preach participates in planning, he is able to give insights on anticipated points of application, songs that fit the meaning of the message, prayer issues that relate to the sermon's topic matter, and Scripture passages that are relevant to the sermon's content. However, the preaching pastor should not be the only one planning worship. In that scenario, the church's worship can often align too closely to the pastor's preferences, leading to an undue repetition of readings and songs. Having an additional planner, particularly one who is attuned to the church's music capacity and traditions, will enrich the planning process.

Together, we plan our church's worship services nearly every week of the year. Brian is the senior pastor of our congregation and in this role serves as the primary preaching pastor. Jason is Brian's pastoral assistant, and his duties include regularly planning and leading the music in the worship gatherings. The two of us meet midweek to plan, and we each prepare for this planning session. Brian develops his sermon outline and makes note of any particularly apt song or Scripture selections. Jason prepares service suggestions based on the text and Brian's outline. These preparations make the planning more efficient; we rarely waste time briskly flipping through a hymnal hoping to find the right song. Even if we discard our prepared suggestions, we are closer to a plan than if we had come to the meeting without having done thoughtful reflection.

An example of our planning process shows how two leaders can collaborate to plan a sermon-serving worship gathering. For a recent service, Brian planned to preach 1 Corinthians 9:1 – 18 under the title "Freed to Preach the Gospel." Brian used the apostle Paul's example to exhort believers to preach the gospel regardless of who you are (verses 1 – 14) and regardless of what you gain (verses 15 – 18). The outline and the sermon text have a strong emphasis on evangelism.

Early in the week, Jason prepared suggestions for the service. This pattern represents our church's typical Sunday morning service, which lasts approximately one hour and fifteen minutes. All hymn numbers represent entries in the 1991 edition of the *Baptist Hymnal.*

Announcements and Welcome
Call to Worship: Psalm 150 (with opening word of prayer)
Hymn 27: "All Creatures of Our God and King"
Hymn 204: "Glorious Is Thy Name"
Scripture Reading: Isaiah 52:7 – 10
Pastoral Prayer
Hymn (inserted in bulletin): "Christ, for the World We Sing"
Hymn (inserted in bulletin): "All I Have Is Christ"
Offertory Prayer
Offertory Music: Psalm 105:1 – 4, set to tune of "It Came Upon the Midnight Clear," led by accompanists and vocalists for the congregation to listen to
Ministry of the Word
Hymn 604: "Come, All Christians, Be Committed"
Moment of Silent Reflection
Closing Prayer
Benediction: Psalm 72:18 – 19

The opening sequence of reading and songs (Psalm 150, Hymn 27, and Hymn 204) gives a foundation for Brian's first sermon point (i.e., "preach the gospel regardless of who you are"). Psalm 150 emphatically commands everything with breath to praise God. Hymn 27 restates that imperative and applies it directly to humanity ("all ye men . . . take your part"). Hymn 204 provides a corporate tone to the task of declaring

God's praises: "Blessed Savior, we adore Thee; we Thy love and grace proclaim."

The next section of the order of worship (Isaiah 52:7–10, Pastoral Prayer, "Christ, for the World We Sing," and "All I Have Is Christ") adds a layer of richness to the theme of evangelism. In hearing Isaiah 52 read, the church is reminded that the Christian act of evangelism is foretold in the Old Testament and described as a beautiful act of service.

A service leader delivers the pastoral prayer, which includes petitions for a number of needs specific to our congregation. This prayer also has an emphasis on our evangelistic faithfulness and fervor.

The next two suggested songs contribute to the evangelistic theme. "Christ, for the World We Sing" is a theologically rich hymn from the *Trinity Hymnal* (#447) and is set to a tune our church recognizes from another song ("Come, Thou Almighty King"). The song fits well with the second point of Brian's sermon (i.e., "preach the gospel regardless of what you gain") by reminding Christians of the "work," "reproach," and "cross to bear" in missions.

"All I Have Is Christ" is a modern hymn that our church enthusiastically enjoys. It connects with the service through a prayerful line, "Use my ransomed life in any way you choose," and contributes a clear articulation of the gospel.

Our offertory prayer and music provide a final moment of preparation and reflection before the sermon. A common practice in our church is listening to a psalm set to a familiar tune. In this instance, Psalm 105 sustains the evangelism focus with its commands to "make known among the nations what he has done " (verse 1) and to "tell of all his wonderful acts" (verse 2).

The song suggested for after the sermon—"Come, All Christians, Be Committed"—is an action-oriented hymn that promotes Christian service. In our typical fashion, we plan a moment to reflect on the service and sermon, a final prayer, and a closing benediction, which is a final pronouncement from God's word. This particular benediction is a prayer that "the whole earth be filled with his glory" (Psalm 72:19).

When we met to plan this particular service, we kept many of these suggestions. We made one change by replacing "Come, All Christians, Be Committed" with the hymn "Soldiers of Christ, in Truth Arrayed" (Hymn 574), which has a stronger evangelism focus than the suggested hymn of response.

The primary advantage of this method of planning is working to ensure that the other worship elements support the preaching of God's word. The proposition of the sermon becomes the pulse for the entire time of worship. The congregation leaves the gathering with a clear sense of the pastor's word-derived counsel for the week ahead.

Read the Word

In many churches, the sermon provides the only moments when God's people hear God's word. However, the New Testament, and specifically the apostle Paul, envisions God's word audibly present throughout Christian worship. Paul commands his protégé, Timothy, to devote himself to "the public reading of Scripture" (1 Timothy 4:13). Interestingly, he gave the command for his letters to receive a similar public audience (Colossians 4:16; 1 Thessalonians 5:27). Since God's word is useful (2 Timothy 3:16), then the reading of Spirit-inspired Scripture from both the Old and New Testaments benefits God's people.

Church leaders should, therefore, incorporate the public reading of God's word in their worship gatherings. The public reading of Scripture can play several roles in the worship service. Through a call to worship, a church leader can read God's word near the beginning of a service to elicit the attention and participation of worshipers. The psalms and other praise-oriented passages—for example, the songs of Hannah (1 Samuel 2:1–10), Mary (Luke 1:46–55), and the heavenly hosts (Revelation 5:9–14; 15:3–4)—exemplify the attitudes, emotions, and thoughts that Christians should have in worship. An appropriate opening passage also introduces key themes that will reoccur throughout the time of worship.

Additional Scripture readings can bring great value to the worship service. Often, a text from a different genre or section of Scripture brings clarity or detail to the sermon passage. For example, if a sermon passage from the New Testament quotes extensively from an Old Testament passage, reading the Old Testament text at some point in the service will allow the preacher to refer to that other text throughout his sermon. Some passages, ranging from the Ten Commandments (Exodus 20:1–17) to prophets' indictments of Israel (Isaiah 1:10–20) to New Testament descriptions of sin (1 John 1:5–10), are particularly effective in preparing the congregation to confess sin. Some passages facilitate times of corporate prayer by modeling prayer (Matthew 6:9–13), commanding prayer (1 Timothy 2:1–2), or showing the effectiveness of prayer (James 5:16–18). Texts that display Christian doctrine in clear and powerful ways, such as John's discussion of the eternality and incarnation of Christ (John 1:1–14) or Paul's definition of the gospel

(1 Corinthians 15:1–8), remind believers of key truths that they must hold to in order to persevere in their faith (1 Corinthians 15:2; 1 Timothy 4:16).

In our service planning, we share a biblical conviction for varying the genre of Scripture readings. A general principle is to choose Scripture readings from the Testament that is not being preached. On occasion, our Scripture readings are from the same Testament as the sermon, but we select a reading from a different genre (e.g., a Scripture reading from the gospels, when the sermon is from the epistles). Varying the readings conveys a confidence in all of God's word as inspired and useful (2 Timothy 3:16). Furthermore, this practice follows the example of our Savior, who articulated the biblical basis of his life, death, and resurrection with a cross section of Old Testament references (Luke 24:44, "the Law of Moses, the Prophets and the Psalms").

A benediction is an appropriate way to end a worship service. Using a short passage of Scripture, a minister dismisses God's people with one final exhortation. The benediction is not a mystical conduit for blessings; instead, it is another strategy for communicating the importance of God's word and emphasizing themes from the sermon and service. Your church's traditional hymnal may have a list of scriptural benedictions, as the *Baptist Hymnal* does (#722). Some of our favorite selections include the following passages.

- "The Lord bless you and keep you; the Lord make his face shine on you and be gracious to you; the Lord turn his countenance toward you and give you peace" (Numbers 6:24–26).

This passage conveys to believers hope and the assurance of God's presence.

- "Praise be to the LORD God, the God of Israel, who alone does marvelous deeds. Praise be to his glorious name forever; may the whole earth be filled with his glory. Amen and Amen" (Psalm 72:18–19).

When we specifically aim to make God's people zealous for his glory, we find this reading an inspiring ending to the service.

- "May the God who gives endurance and encouragement give you the same attitude of mind toward each other that Christ Jesus had, so that with one mind and one voice you may glorify the God and Father of our Lord Jesus Christ" (Romans 15:5–6).

This Pauline prayer punctuates services that emphasize Christian unity.

- "The grace of the Lord Jesus Christ, and the love of God, and the fellowship of the Holy Spirit be with you all" (2 Corinthians 13:14).

This succinct reading that affirms the doctrine of the Trinity and speaks of fundamental Christian experiences (e.g., "grace," "love," and "fellowship") is a fitting conclusion to any worship service.

- "May God himself, the God of peace, sanctify you through and through. May your whole spirit, soul and body be kept blameless at the coming of our Lord Jesus Christ. The one who calls you is faithful, and he will do it" (1 Thessalonians 5:23–24).

For sermons and services that focus on Christian

sanctification, this benediction sustains that focus, while reminding God's people of his faithfulness.

- "May the Lord direct your hearts into God's love and Christ's perseverance" (2 Thessalonians 3:5).

  When the preached word summons believers to endure trials, this benediction provides a simple, strongly worded prayer.

- "Now may the God of peace, who through the blood of the eternal covenant brought back from the dead our Lord Jesus, that great Shepherd of the sheep, equip you with everything good for doing his will, and may he work in us what is pleasing to him, through Jesus Christ, to whom be glory for ever and ever. Amen" (Hebrews 13:20–21).

  This reading fittingly concludes services exulting in the work of Christ on the cross, specifically after the worshipers have celebrated the Lord's Supper.

Pray the Word

Corporate prayer finds both its charge and content in God's word. The commands and examples of Scripture give believers a full agenda for prayer, and the public gathering is an apt time and place for practicing the discipline of prayer. Basic human needs, such as the provision of food (Matthew 6:11) and good health (3 John 2), should be matters of prayer. Christians pray for the conversion and salvation of others (Romans 10:1). Other believers and their growth in godliness are high priorities for prayer, as the apostle Paul shows when he prays for Christians' unity (Romans 15:5–6); hope, joy, and peace (Romans 15:13);

experience of grace (1 Corinthians 16:23); wisdom, revelation, and knowledge (Ephesians 1:16–17); increased love and spiritual fruit (Philippians 1:9–11); and endurance and patience (Colossians 1:11–12). When fellow believers suffer crises, such as threatening illnesses, Christians pray for them (James 5:14–15). God's people confess their sins to each other (James 5:16) and, through prayer, to God (Daniel 9:4–5).

Christian ministers greatly need the prayers of those in their charge and of likeminded believers in other congregations. The apostle Paul's frequent prayer requests are a good guide in praying for gospel ministers. Christians should pray for ministers to have boldness in declaring the gospel (Ephesians 6:18–19), opportunities to declare Christ (Colossians 4:2), favorable reception of their messages (2 Thessalonians 3:1), and deliverance from persecutors (2 Thessalonians 3:2). Christians are admonished to pray for authorities, specifically that their leadership will allow Christians to live lives that are "peaceful and quiet" (1 Timothy 2:1–2).

The local gathering represents an occasion for obeying these commands. More importantly, neglecting the practice of corporate prayer stands in violation of God's word (1 Timothy 2:8). Since the calling of ministry entails a devotion to prayer (Acts 6:4), pastors must lead their congregations to embrace corporate prayer. Each local church should have a pastor-led, congregation-supported strategy for corporate prayer that includes times for focused and extended prayer. Each formal public gathering of God's people must have a time of prayer.

A wise consideration is to vary the approach to prayer in these gatherings. For example, if a church has several gatherings a week (e.g., a Sunday morning service, Sunday evening service, Wednesday night service), the time and type of prayer can vary in these services. At our church, a pastor leads prayers during the morning service, using his awareness of the congregation's needs to inform his prayer. During the evening service, in an extended prayer time, a pastor gives the congregation details on matters of prayer and members are called on to pray. In our Wednesday night setting, members mention prayer requests, and volunteers pray for categories of requests. This variety benefits our congregation in many ways. Our services and the intentionality in our prayer strategy communicate the importance and necessity of prayer. Members know they are being prayed for. Pastor-led prayers give members examples to follow in their own private and public prayers. Having opportunities to pray publically helps members feel involved in the life of our church. Congregations can vary their approach to corporate prayer based on a number of factors (e.g., size, maturity of members), but they must not neglect this discipline.

A part of our prayer strategy is a focused, pastor-led prayer during the morning service. The focus of the prayer depends on the themes of the sermon and service. The most common focused prayer times are pastoral prayers and prayers of confession. A pastoral prayer addresses ongoing pressing needs of the congregation. Requests often relate to basic needs, health concerns, family changes (e.g., marriages, births), and particularly difficult trials. A prayer of confession—often planned when sermons have extensive applications related to obedience and sanctification—addresses sinful attitudes, beliefs, behaviors, and emotions. The praying pastor describes specific sins, pleads for God's forgiveness, and reflects on the gospel's power and victory over these sins. Other focused, pastor-led prayers have included prayers dedicated to the persecuted church, the unconverted, and civil authorities. These themes emerged because of their relevance to content of the sermon and the biblical warrant for praying through these issues.

Sing the Word

As with prayer, Scripture insists on and informs congregational singing. Church leaders can look to a variety of sources for guidance in their worship ministries—blogs, conferences, magazines, and popular contemporary Christian music. Before leaders consider the advice of these sources, they need a framework for the Bible's instructions on congregational singing. All of a church's decisions on song selection and styles must pass through this filter. Biblical faithfulness is the single most important criterion for church leaders to consider.

A seminal text on congregational singing is Ephesians 5:19. This admonishment was clearly an important part of Paul's vision for the local church because he repeats the same encouragement to the church at Colossae (Colossians 3:16). In the context of Ephesians 5, Paul's instruction regarding congregational singing fills out his charge to the Ephesians that they should live wisely and watch their walk (Ephesians 5:15). Specifically, verse 19 gives detail to the command "be filled with the Spirit" (verse 18). Paul envisions believers "addressing one another in psalms and hymns and spiritual songs, singing and making melody to the Lord with your heart" (verse 19 ESV).

This text teaches about the audience of corporate worship.

An often repeated and well-meaning worship cliché is that worship has one audience, God. However, Paul identifies two audiences. Congregational singing has vertical and horizontal dimensions. On the one hand, Christians direct their singing upward to God, "making melody to the Lord." Yet, Christians also sing outward to each other; they address one another "in psalms and hymns and spiritual songs." In subsequent chapters, we will apply this dual-audience concept to a variety of issues, including selecting songs and leading singing. Before all the practical decisions, though, come the understanding and acceptance that Christian worship is a vehicle for mutual edification instead of simply being an insular, emotional connection with God. As Christians sing, they address each other, reminding one another of their commonly held truths in order to spur one another on in a wise, Spirit-filled, God-honoring walk with the Lord.

The text provides insight into the content of congregational singing. The apostle Paul describes it as "psalms and hymns and spiritual songs." Interestingly, Paul would have the Ephesians sing Scripture, specifically, the Old Testament psalms. Though "psalms" had a broad use in the Greco-Roman world, early Christians most likely understood Paul to refer to the psalms of the Old Testament. Early church figures, such as Tertullian, Eusebius of Caesarea, Athanasius, Augustine, Jerome, and Saint Sidonius Apollinaris, make reference to the practice of Old Testament psalm singing in the early church.[2] Paul's words, here in Ephesians 5, demand that the God-breathed expressions of praise from the book of Psalms make their way into churches' repertoires of songs. For guidance on introducing psalm singing to your church, see appendix 1, "Reintroducing Psalm Singing."

Paul does not impose on Christians the command to sing psalms *exclusively*. His reference to "hymns and spiritual songs" legitimizes other musical expressions of the church's doctrine. Paul obeyed his own command to make use of other kinds of songs. In a few instances, Paul cites early Christian poetry—perhaps the vestiges of early Christian hymnody—in his teaching (Philippians 2:5–11; 2 Timothy 2:11–13). Furthermore, the worship scenes in Revelation show God's people singing new songs and texts not found elsewhere in Scripture (Revelation 4:11; 5:9–10; 19:6–8). To demand that only Old Testament psalms be sung in the gatherings of the church is a misconstruction of Paul's words in Ephesians 5 and Colossians 3 and the broader example of the New Testament. However, "hymns and spiritual songs" does not provide carte blanche for church leaders to import just anything into their music rotation. Recall that Paul's hymn citations fit rather seamlessly alongside Scripture. "Hymns and spiritual songs" are biblical in their content. They should articulate Christian doctrines and elicit expressly Christian virtues, especially considering that Christians address them to one another for the purpose of encouragement.

These principles—that congregational singing has a dual audience and that congregational singing is biblical in its content—constitute a cease-fire directive for the "worship wars." Congregations that cast a suspicious eye toward contemporary spiritual songs without first examining their content have not grasped the dual-audience concept. A similar problem persists among those congregations that cast off traditional hymns as antiquated. Both of these worship warriors have an audience of one—themselves. Seeing mutual edification as a purpose of congregational singing and considering others more important than ourselves should lead Christians in multigenerational churches to sing with gladness a range of songs and styles.

A multitude of historic hymns are well suited for honoring God and encouraging other believers. Similarly, an increasing number of contemporary spiritual songs or "modern hymns," as we call them, are equally well suited for these tasks. Each church needs to exercise wisdom in balancing the benefits of a multigenerational hymnody. Our congregation, which includes a significant percentage of members who are accustomed to historic hymns, approaches the issue by singing songs with good content from a trustworthy hymnal and supplementing doctrinally rich and easily learned modern hymns. This method has contributed to a healthy worship environment for a church made up of people from multiple cultures and generations.

See the Word

The ordinances of baptism and the Lord's Supper are important elements of Christian worship.* These two practices were instituted under the divine authority of Jesus Christ. The

*Throughout this book, we discuss the ordinances from our perspective and tradition. We recognize that some readers have different views on the meaning and modes of these ordinances, as well as on who are the proper recipients of these ordinances. Instead of attempting to persuade readers of our convictions, we encourage readers to consider our recommendations in the context of their own views.

Christian ordinance of baptism is part of the enduring mission of the church (Matthew 28:18–20). After unbelievers are converted to Christ, they receive the ordinance of baptism from a local congregation of believers by being submerged in water and raised out of it. Baptism is deeply symbolic of conversion, salvation, and union with Christ (Romans 6:1–4). Thus, the practice depicts to all who see it that sinful humans can receive the benefits of Christ's death and anticipate the glory of a resurrection that is like Christ's own.

Similarly, Jesus Christ instituted the Lord's Supper and expected that Christians would repeat the practice throughout the ages (1 Corinthians 11:23–26). Christians participate in the Lord's Supper by eating bread and drinking juice from a cup. These elements are wonderfully symbolic of Christ's death for sins. Just as Christ broke the bread and distributed it at the first Lord's Supper, so he also freely gave of his body for the benefit of those who believe. As one pours a drink into his mouth from a cup, so also Christ poured out his blood to achieve the forgiveness of sins. When congregations partake of the Lord's Supper, they strikingly "proclaim the Lord's death" (1 Corinthians 11:26).

Ministers must administer these ordinances in worshipful ways. They should exhaustively teach about the ordinances in their preaching ministries and briefly summarize the meaning of the ordinances when administering them. The congregation should know in advance that the ordinances will be administered so they can thoughtfully prepare. The significance of the ordinances deserves emphasis and protection. One way of protecting the ordinances' significance is by prohibiting private participation in the ordinances. Since baptism and the Lord's Supper visually remind Christians of the gospel and conversion, the whole congregation should experience these worshipful moments together. A baptism is too edifying and meaningful for a pool at youth camp; let the whole congregation receive the visual encouragement of a young soul that has passed from death to life! Another prudent protection is to limit the role of the visual arts in worship. Baptism and the Lord's Supper are the visual depictions of the Christian faith that God has explicitly ordained. Certainly, expressions of dramatic and visual arts are often beautiful and soul nourishing, but their presence in congregational worship gatherings can be duplicative and distracting.

Conclusion

These practices are the central elements of worship: the preaching of God's word, the public reading of God's word, praying in accordance with God's word, singing what coheres with God's word, and seeing God's word through the ordinances. God has graciously blessed his people by taking great care to teach them how to glorify him in worship. He has told us not only what to do in worship but also how to do it. In Christian worship, as with all aspects of the Christian life, may we learn to "not go beyond what is written" (1 Corinthians 4:6).

CHAPTER 3

SPIRITUALITY OF WORSHIP

WORSHIP PLANNERS are particularly susceptible to ruts in their selection of service elements. Congregations tend to develop an informal liturgy in which a few dozen songs are rotated throughout the year. Another tendency is to conform worship services to preconceived, ambiguous notions of flow, pacing, or tempo. The first song is invariably upbeat and joyfully expressive. At least one song of the gathering is somber, and the service immediately transitions to a more triumphant tone. The final song of the morning is oriented toward either commitment or joy. As they develop an order of worship, the worship planning team discards suggested songs because they do not "feel like a second song." An unfortunate consequence of these trends is a failure to model and teach how believers should feel.

A few years ago, we were powerfully reminded of the importance of emotions in worship planning. Each December, our church focuses on Christ's incarnation in our teaching and worship. For the first Sunday of the month, we planned a service with selections intended to encourage hope and elicit joy. Some of the songs included "Come, Thou Long-Expected

Jesus"; "O Come, All Ye Faithful"; and "Good Christian Men, Rejoice." The events of that week, however, tested the resilience of our hope and joy. Another like-minded congregation with connections to our church lost its pastor and his wife in a car accident. This pastor had mentored several men in our church, and our church as a whole was fond of him and his wife. Only a couple days later, one of our church's deacons, who was married and had two young children, lost his life in a car accident. Grief overwhelmed our entire church.

How should a church respond to these tragedies as it gathers for worship? Sticking to the plan—as though the congregation should suppress its sorrow and sing, "Rejoice with heart and soul and voice! Now ye hear of endless bliss"—would egregiously fail to lead and serve God's people. We revised our plans and began our service with tender expressions of grief and comfort. Worship began with a reading from Psalm 23, a somberly sung paraphrase of that passage ("My Shepherd Will Supply My Need"), and a musical plea for God's nearness ("Abide with Me"). From these intensely emotional elements, we eventually transitioned to more hopeful Scripture readings and songs. However, if the service had begun with these expressions of hope, our worship would have been disingenuous. Acknowledging the grief and shepherding our congregation through sorrow were essential pastoral responsibilities.

Simply stated, biblical spirituality includes a range of emotions, and Christian worship should too. This chapter explores how the psalms can provide an emotional model for Christian living and corporate worship. Taking our cues from the psalms, we will consider how to reflect biblical spirituality in worship planning and also give specific examples of emotionally varied worship gatherings.

The Psalms as an Emotional Model

In our experience, Christians are often too dismissive of emotions. A well-meaning Christian may counsel a friend not to let his emotions get the best of him. Even an otherwise mature believer may refuse to admit her emotions to others for fear of criticism. An unhelpful view of the emotions as an uncontrollable force pervades many pockets of evangelicalism. Consider, however, that the psalms, which are wholly true because of God's work of inspiration, strongly convey a variety of emotions.

Few forms of poetry have ever expressed *exuberance* quite like the psalms. The psalmists often forcefully call their readers to joy. "Be glad in the Lord," commands David, "and rejoice, O righteous, and shout for joy, all you upright in heart!" (Psalm 32:11 ESV). That one verse has three commands—"be glad," "rejoice," and "shout for joy"—for God's people to exude happiness. The joy of the psalmists is greater than earthly joys, such as material possessions (Psalm 4:7), culinary delicacies (Psalm 63:5), and the comfort of rest (Psalm 149:5).

The psalmists frequently voice their *exasperation*. They ask frank and seemingly irreverent questions of God: "Lord, where is your former great love?" (Psalm 89:49). "How long, Lord? Will you forget me forever?" (Psalm 13:1). "Why, Lord, do you stand far off?" (Psalm 10:1). "Who will bring me . . . ? Who will lead me . . . ?" (Psalm 60:9). "What profit is there if I am silenced, if I go down to the pit?" (Psalm 30:9). The people of God are not stoically calm in the midst of suffering; rather, they express their anguish honestly and openly before God.

Confession of sin is a powerful emotional motif in the book of Psalms. David compares his feelings of conviction and guilt to the startling image of broken bones (Psalm 51:8) and the intensity of a summer drought (Psalm 32:4). The extent to which the psalms speak of sin is clear from the apostle Paul's letter to the Romans. When he defends his claim that all people are "under the power of sin" (Romans 3:9–10), he cites six selections from various sections of the Psalter. The psalmists forthrightly admit their guilt (Psalm 32:5; 41:4; 51:4; 106:6), and they are eager for God to "have mercy on" and "heal" them (Psalm 41:4), "take away" all their sins (Psalm 25:18), and "restore" (Psalm 51:12) them.

The psalms encourage believers with their declarations of *confidence* in God. The psalmists see God as limitlessly sovereign, doing whatever he pleases (Psalm 115:3). He is "the great King over all the earth" (Psalm 47:2), to whom all other powers are subject (Psalm 47:9). His powerful voice created all things (Psalm 33:6, 9), and with a mere word, he can accomplish his will in the world (Psalms 107:20; 147:15, 18). God's great power inspires confident praises from his people. He is their "refuge" (Psalm 91:9), "stronghold" (Psalm 27:1), "fortress" (Psalm 18:2), "Rock" (Psalm 144:1), "shield" (Psalm 3:3), and "help" (Psalm 121:1–2). Therefore, God's people refuse to fear moral or natural evil (Psalm 91:3–10).

Reflecting Spirituality in Planning

These examples from the book of Psalms show God's people expressing their emotions as they worship him. Christian leaders defy these examples when they make joy the central and exclusive emotional response in their worship gatherings. Following after Christ is an experience of joy, but that joy often comes through the consolation of "the God of all comfort, who comforts us in all our troubles" (2 Corinthians 1:3–4). If a church's only reference to Christians' feelings of despondency and exasperation is the upbeat song "Trading My Sorrows," which speaks of turning our pain and sorrow into joy and gladness, then something has gone awry in its pursuit of biblical worship.

Many congregations foster expressions of emotion in their worship. Common expressions include clapping, raising hands, shouting, and dancing, and each has a varying degree of biblical attestation. However, leaders should not confuse the presence of these expressions with a healthy emotional life in the church. Many of the emotions we see modeled in the book of Psalms and in other portions of Scripture do not have an obvious physical manifestation. In planning worship, leaders in these churches need occasionally to incorporate choices that lead the congregation toward heart clenching instead of hand raising. Every church can improve on how it emotionally leads its members.

Worship planners should give careful consideration to the emotions they want their congregations to experience. Unfortunately, many Christians have only experienced this kind of emotive leadership in services that aim at forcing decisions from unbelievers. Reflecting biblical spirituality does not mean that worship planners should manipulate the emotions of those participating in worship. Instead, local church leaders should contemplate which emotional responses are germane to the content of the sermon. The selection of service elements should reflect how Christians ought to feel in light of the doctrine and application embodied in the preaching.

At our church, we often construct services to elicit joy in believers. Our celebrations of incarnation each December and Easter each spring are times of unrestrained joy. Similarly, when a sermon text dwells on the good news of salvation, we aim to enliven the Godward affections of our church. The gospel message—that Christ was born, lived a sinless life, died for sins, and rose from the grave—prompts assurance, confidence, delight, hope, and joy in Christians. In services with joyful themes, we open with call-to-worship texts that model joy in God, including Psalm 16:9 ("my heart is glad"), Psalm 96:11 ("Let the heavens rejoice, let the earth be glad"), Psalm 100:1 ("Shout for joy to the Lord"), and Psalm 136 ("his love endures forever," a refrain repeated in each verse). For these exultant gatherers, we are fond of triumphant hymns, such as "Rejoice, the Lord Is King," "Come, Christians, Join to Sing," "And Can It Be," "Ye, Servants of God," and "All Hail the Power of Jesus' Name."

Several times each year, we plan services with intentionally somber elements. Typically, one Sunday morning in December, we create a worship gathering that simulates Israel's anticipation of the coming Messiah. Readings like Psalm 62:1 ("For God alone my soul waits in silence," ESV) and hymns like "O Come, O Come, Emmanuel" connect believers emotionally with Israel's dejection in its captivity and remind Christians how we should await Christ's return. The Sunday before Easter, we sometimes lead a service that mournfully considers

Christ's death. Portions of Psalm 22, Isaiah 53, and the gospels' crucifixion accounts—along with hymns like "When I Survey the Wondrous Cross," "Alas, and Did My Savior Bleed," "What Wondrous Love Is This," "'Man of Sorrows,' What a Name," and "In Christ Alone"—drive home the significance of Jesus' suffering.

A few times a year, we have worship gatherings that focus on confession and repentance. Our aim is to communicate both the reality of our sins and the availability of forgiveness in Christ. We lead our church toward repentance with deliberately somber elements, such as readings from Psalm 51, Psalm 139:23–24, and Isaiah 1:10–20 and songs like "Search Me, O God," "Jesus, I Come," and "I Saw the Cross of Jesus." We have found it helpful and necessary to elevate our congregation's sense of assurance by transitioning to clear expressions of forgiveness found in hymns like "There Is a Fountain," "Grace Greater Than Our Sin," and "Before the Throne of God Above."

Churches take different approaches to the difficult task of service planning. However, by virtue of our common faith in Christ and obligation to God's word, and despite our divergent cultural settings, churches will have remarkable similarities. All true Christian churches will preach God's word, sing praises to God, offer prayers, and observe the ordinances. A regard for biblical spirituality deserves a place among these time-tested, word-mandated worship practices.

Conclusion

The first Sunday of every December, many in our church are mindful of the grief we shared several years ago. Those difficult days always starkly contrast with the joy we find in Christ's incarnation. Yet, that joy is the only means we have for truly grieving the loss of our friends. A few months after these tragedies, we debuted a new song in our worship repertoire. "To Live Is Christ," from Sovereign Grace Music, served us well as we learned to "not grieve like the rest of mankind, who have no hope" (1 Thessalonians 4:13).

As you reflect on what you've read in this chapter and ponder the lyrics below, our prayer for you, as a minister of God's people, is that you will faithfully lead God's people to love God with all of their heart, soul, and might, even in the midst of heartbreaking, soul-crushing, might-depleting loss.

Before You gave us life and breath
You numbered all our days
You set Your gracious love on us
And chose us to be saved
This fleeting life is passing by
With all its joys and pain
But we believe to live is Christ
And death is gain

[Chorus] To live is Christ, to die is gain
In every age this truth remains
We will not fear, we're unashamed
To live is Christ, to die is gain
To live is Christ, to die is gain

And though we grieve for those we love
Who fall asleep in Christ
We know they'll see the Savior's face

And gaze into His eyes
So now we grieve, yet we don't grieve
As those who have no hope
For just as Jesus rose again
He'll raise His own

And now we're longing for the day
We'll see the Lamb once slain
Who saved a countless multitude
To glorify His name
We're yearning for the wedding feast
Of Jesus and His bride
His nail-scarred hands will finally
Bring us to His side[3]

PART 2

PLAN WORSHIP

CHAPTER 4

PLANNING THE READING OF THE WORD

EACH YEAR, OUR CHURCH PROVIDES several opportunities for seminary students to become involved in a pastoral internship. One requirement is to take part in a worship planning session. Interns are often impressed with our ability to recall the lyrics and page numbers of entries in our church's hymnal. Yet, this knack comes to almost anyone who weekly plans worship services. We grow so accustomed to the available worship materials that little facts about songs are firmly planted in our minds. Our favorite way of showing off is to use hymn titles (e.g., #339, "Not What My Hands Have Done") to indicate gas prices (e.g., $3.39 per gallon).

The best way to improve worship planning skills is to plan services regularly. Learning how to plan worship services comes mostly through trial and error. Consider an instance where leaders at a local church noticed that the congregation did not sing loudly during a recent service. As they think through the issue, they may come to realize that many of the songs they are using are unfamiliar, the arrangements are too dissimilar from the church's tradition, or the amplification of the instrumentalists and vocalists is overpowering.

In addition to learning from their mistakes, church leaders should learn to utilize a few tools in the planning process. Planning from memory may be convenient, but the approach has its flaws too. Without a deliberate process for planning, church leaders' whims will become the norm for the church's worship. Since most of us gravitate toward the familiar, worship planning by the whim results in undue repetition of readings, prayer emphases, and song selections. However, if we are seeking to equip God's people for works of service (Ephesians 4:11 – 12), we need gatherings that are theologically robust and doctrinally multifaceted—where the whole will of God is proclaimed (Acts 20:27), not just reshuffled tidbits. This chapter provides criteria, resources, and examples for church leaders to spur on their congregations toward Christian maturity, to what Paul calls, "the whole measure of the fullness of Christ" (Ephesians 4:13). Specifically, our focus is on planning Scripture readings, corporate prayer, and worship music.

Criteria for Scripture Readings

We have previously argued that the New Testament commands and commends the public reading of Scripture. Paul insists that his protégés and their congregations read aloud what the Spirit-inspired prophets of the Old and New Testament ages inscripturated (Colossians 4:16; 1 Thessalonians 5:27; 1 Timothy 4:13).

Our Sunday morning gathering—which is the only formal activity of our church that we insist members attend—

typically features three readings from God's word. A call to worship begins our time of corporate worship; a mid-service Scripture reading sustains and steers the theme of the service; and a benediction dismisses our congregation with one final exhortation from the Scriptures.

We use several criteria in planning these public readings. The chief consideration is coherence with the content of the sermon. Using the outline of the sermon and motifs of the sermon passage, we identify a few themes that relate to what the congregation will hear during the ministry of the word. Themes are as simple as one-word descriptions like *wisdom.* Themes can be as formal as a doctrinal description like *substitutionary atonement*, or as focused as a Christian discipline like *prayer.* As we consider each other's suggestions for the service, we identify connections with these broad themes. Ask us on any given Sunday, and we should be able to provide the thematic rationale for our Scripture reading selections.

Compatibility with the sermon is not the only consideration. Scripture readings should represent a diversity of Testaments and genres. Our regular pattern is to choose a psalm for the call to worship and to choose a passage from the Testament not being preached for the Scripture reading. As we previously stated, readings from a variety of genres enlighten God's people and follow our Lord's example.

Scripture readings also provide natural points of transition in the service. Certain texts prepare God's people for specific actions. If we plan for our church to pray corporately for needs or to confess sin, a Scripture reading can set our minds toward these tasks. Often, reading Scripture before baptism can reiterate the meaning of the ordinance in a way that encourages believers and instructs unbelievers. Scripture readings can also bring closure to sections of the service. After prayers of confession, for example, a reading from God's word can powerfully communicate to Christians the realities of redemption and forgiveness of sins. Effective "word of assurance" texts include Romans 8:1; 1 Corinthians 6:11; and 1 John 1:8–9. This service element is a blessing and reassurance for all believers, especially for those with a tender conscience who deeply feel the wounds of their sin.

Practicalities of Scripture Readings

A few practicalities are important in the selection of Scripture readings. The length of readings is one issue that requires wisdom and pastoral sensitivity. A passage of more than a dozen verses sometimes tries the patience of congregations. Long readings could be a long-term goal for your church; make sure to lay the foundation by teaching about the importance of Scripture reading, modeling confidence in God's word, and gradually incorporating longer readings. On the other hand, short portions of Scripture can be effective, but worship planners must give appropriate regard for context. Do no hermeneutical harm to your congregation's understanding of Scripture.

Assessing the content of readings requires discernment. All Scripture is useful, but because of the noetic effects of sin, all passages do not profit us as they should. If Peter could call some of Paul's writings hard to understand (2 Peter 3:16)—as Shakespeare's iteration of Ulysses says, "The raven chides blackness"—we should not pretend all passages are alike in their clarity. Readings replete with difficult Hebrew names (e.g., genealogies) or with extended, complicated analogies (e.g., the comparison of Moses' covenantal ceremony with Christ's new covenant inauguration in Hebrews 9) may pose too great a challenge for our hearers. One way of analyzing the clarity of a reading is to ask, "Will the congregation make the connection between this passage and the sermon?"

Resources for Scripture Readings

Several resources help us find readings that are diverse in genre, practical for recitation, and relevant to the sermon. A quality study Bible is a good starting place. Cross-references reliably show a passage's allusions to and intertextual relationships with other portions of Scripture. If a New Testament passage explicitly quotes an Old Testament text, or if a New Testament text plainly shows the fulfillment of an Old Testament passage, these intertestamental connections can prove useful for Scripture reading choices.

Concordances are useful tools for planning. Searching for keywords related to central themes from the sermon will yield many options for Scripture readings. Online concordances have advanced search options that help planners identify readings from diverse genres. Often, we find our call to worship texts by searching for keywords in the book of Psalms. For instance, for a sermon that focuses on church unity, a keyword search for the word *unity* will take planners to Psalm 133, which celebrates the times "when God's people live together in unity" (verse 1). A search for *congregation* leads to Psalm 22, which speaks of declaring God's name in "the midst of the congregation" to "brothers" (verse 22 ESV). Planners must utilize this tool with care and wisdom. Keyword searches can lead to texts that do not have a clear connection to the sermon passage. Worse yet, we can draw verses out of their context, distort their meaning, and confuse the congregation. Worship planners must give priority to correctly handling the word of truth (2 Timothy 2:15) as they choose readings.

We recommend that planners keep records of their selections. Various record-keeping tools exist, from online worship planning software to old-fashioned pen and paper. We use a simple spreadsheet with tabs for tracking selected songs and readings. Planners can consult these records to avoid frequent repetition of readings. Our preference is to avoid repeating reading selections within the quarter of a year (i.e., every three months). By avoiding repetition, we expose our congregation to more than thirty different passages in any given quarter through our calls to worship, Scripture readings, and benedictions. This exposure communicates a confidence and respect for all of God's word. Since this pattern is a mere preference, we do not hesitate to repeat a passage if it is particularly well suited for a service.

Over the years, we have found that our own exercise of personal spiritual disciplines has enhanced our worship planning. Frequently, we come across a passage in our devotional Bible reading that influences sermon preparation and worship planning. When our individual pursuit of knowing God through his word coincides with the ministry of the word at our church, we attribute it to God's meticulous care for his people. A caution that all worship planners must heed, however, is to avoid conflating worship planning and personal spiritual disciplines. Continue to set aside time to read God's word for your own personal benefit, and rejoice when God uses your individual worship to fuel the church's corporate worship.

Examples of Scripture Readings

Using these criteria and resources, we plan Scripture readings that draw people's attention to the preaching of God's word. The ministry of the word at our church consists of expositional, passage-by-passage preaching of whole books of the Bible. Those who preach God's word in this way may wonder how all these principles fit together on a week-to-week basis. What follows are a few examples of sermon passages and the supportive Scripture readings we selected.

An extended section of 1 Corinthians, chapters 8–10, deals with Christian liberties and issues of conscience. As Brian approached the last section of chapter 10 (verses 23–33), he developed a sermon focused on the call for Christians to glorify God (verse 31) with their consciences by seeking the good of other believers (verses 23–30) and the salvation of unbelievers (verses 31–33). We used the general themes of "glorifying God" and "loving others" to identify potential service elements. One option for the opening Scripture reading was Psalm 24, from which Paul quotes: "The earth is the Lord's and everything in it" (Psalm 24:1; 1 Corinthians 10:26). Keyword searches for *glorify* and *glory* in the book of Psalms led us to a few other options. Eventually, we settled on Psalm 86:8–13 for the call to worship because it made several connections with the sermon passage. Just as Paul encouraged believers to take part with thanksgiving (1 Corinthians 10:30) and do so in a way that glorifies God (1 Corinthians 10:31), the psalmist "gives thanks" to God with his "whole heart" and pledges to "glorify" God's name forever (Psalm 86:12 ESV). This section of Psalm 86 also had a reference to all nations glorifying God (verse 9), which connects with an evangelistic application in the sermon. Another thematic advantage of Psalm 86 is its many general lines of praise. Expressions like "there is none like you" (verse 8) and "you are great" (verse 10) model for believers ways to praise God.

The broad theme of "loving others" shaped the second Scripture reading of the service. Paul commands the Corinthians not to seek their own good, but "the good of others" (1 Corinthians 10:24). A couple of options came to mind, including Micah 6, which describes the good that God requires as "justice" and "mercy" and what Christ establishes as the second greatest commandment—loving our neighbors. Since the sermon was from the New Testament, we desired a reading from the Old Testament. When we looked more closely at the "love of neighbor" passage Jesus quotes (Leviticus 19:9–18), we saw some interesting examples of seeking the good of others. Israelites were expected to treat others justly and generously, even leaving some of the harvest for the less fortunate. Finding readings from the Old Testament law that are accessible for public reading is often challenging. Therefore, when we found a relevant passage from the law, we took the opportunity to diversify our public reading of Scripture.

For the final Scripture reading of the day, the concluding

benediction, we chose a praise of Christ from Revelation. All creatures say of God's Son, "To him who sits on the throne and to the Lamb be praise and honor and glory and power for ever and ever!" (Revelation 5:13). This final praise summarized our service well. The sermon challenged God's people to glorify him in everything they do, and the benedictory passage pronounces God's glory. In addition, we celebrated the Lord's Supper after the sermon and sang a hymn that reflects on Christ's sacrifice. That the praises of Revelation 5 are directed toward "the Lamb" solidified for us the choice of benediction.

Planning Scripture readings when the sermon is from the Old Testament can be a challenge. We found this to be true as Brian preached through 1 and 2 Samuel in the last few years. For approximately fifty services, we dealt with themes of kingship, suffering, and God's promises. As Brian approached the end of 2 Samuel, he came to the passage about David's mighty men (2 Samuel 23:8–39). Brian noted characteristics of David's elite force that are also true for Christians. Both are divinely empowered, sacrificially courageous, and faithful in service. Searching for the theme of strength in Psalms led us to select Psalm 28 for the call to worship. David calls God his "Rock," "strength," and "shield" (verses 1, 7). The song concludes with these fortifying promises: "The Lord is the strength of his people, a fortress of salvation for his anointed one" (verse 8).

For the second Scripture reading of the service, we desired a New Testament passage because the sermon was based on an Old Testament passage. We thought of examples of strength, courage, and faithfulness in the New Testament. Martyrdom is perhaps the greatest Christian display of Spirit-enabled might. The reading of Hebrews 10:32–39 allowed us to apply and compare the characteristics of David's mighty men to the confidence (verse 35), endurance (verse 36), and joyful submission to suffering (verse 34) of Christian martyrs. An additional benefit of this reading is that it transitioned our thinking to martyrdom, which segued into a pastor-led prayer for the persecuted church.

The benediction for the service came from Psalm 29. The majority of our benediction texts come from the New Testament. The epistles often conclude with prayers that make for fitting conclusions to services. However, after some research in the concordance, we identified many passages from the Psalms that prayerfully pronounce blessings on God's people. The conclusion of Psalm 29 cohered well with the themes of this particular service: "The Lord gives strength to his people; the Lord blesses his people with peace."

CHAPTER 5

PLANNING THE PRAYING OF THE WORD

IN CHAPTER 2, we described corporate prayer as mandated in and modeled by the New Testament. Neglecting the practice of prayer in the worship gathering is unhelpful to God's people and unfaithful to God's design for Christian worship. How each church sustains its corporate prayer life will vary, based on factors such as size, maturity, and giftedness. Our church uses the different gatherings of the week (i.e., Sunday morning, Sunday evening, and Wednesday evening) to facilitate unique times of prayer. Our main worship gathering on Sunday morning features prayers led by pastors and other leaders in our church. One of these services typically includes four prayers: an opening prayer after the call to worship Scripture reading, a mid-service prayer following a Scripture reading, a prayer prior to our offertory, and a concluding prayer that precedes the benediction.

Three of these prayers have similar content each week. The opening prayer is praise oriented and sets the tone for the rest of the service. In addition, the leader of this prayer usually prays for the congregation and its participation in the service. A prayer before the offertory has themes of thanksgiving and praise. The one voicing this prayer typically intercedes for our church as we give—that we would do so generously and joyfully. The concluding prayer emphasizes our belief in and obedience to the things we have heard from God's word throughout the service. On the other hand, our mid-service prayer varies weekly. We use this time of prayer strategically to address particular issues and themes. The New Testament's commands for prayer dictate the focus of these prayers.

Varieties of Corporate Prayer

One version of the mid-service prayer is the *pastoral prayer*. The leader of this prayer intercedes on behalf of believers in our congregation who have specific needs. In this moment of the service, we mourn with those who mourn by interceding for believers who, for example, are suffering because of illness, the loss of a loved one, or financial peril. We rejoice with those who rejoice by thanking God for recent provisions of his grace, such as new marriages, newborn babies, recoveries from illnesses, and conversions of unbelievers. Frequently, the Scripture reading that occurs prior to this prayer influences the content of the prayer. For instance, if the Scripture reading emphasizes loving one another, the one leading the prayer will ask God to grant our church unity, harmony, and like-mindedness.

A *prayer of confession* is another common focus for the mid-service prayer. This prayer leads God's people to recognize and experience godly sorrow over their sins. The leader of this prayer mentions specific sins that often relate to the application of the sermon and the content of the preceding Scripture reading. The one leading the prayer models biblical confession and repentance. We value public prayers of confession because they lead the church to practice a vital spiritual discipline. In addition, prayers of confession protect the church from clichéd criticisms. Local churches are often derided as being "full of hypocrites," but the accusation loses its potency when God's people openly admit their sinfulness. The authenticity of local churches is often questioned when unbelievers claim that Christians pretend they have no problems. However, the prayer of confession allows us to own up to our inherent flaws and foibles.

The majority of the mid-service prayers are pastoral and confessional. However, over the years, we have incorporated more specific thematic prayers. We have led our church through prayers for other ministries, missionaries, martyrs, the unborn, the unconverted, and civil authorities. These thematic emphases are helpful ways of obeying New Testament prayer commands and of calling attention to important issues in our city and larger culture.

Criteria for Corporate Prayer

Several criteria inform the planning of this mid-service prayer. As with other service elements, the first priority is compatibility with the content of the sermon. The general method is to filter the themes of the sermon through the prayers commanded and modeled in the New Testament. Certain sermon themes evoke responses of dependence and trust, and worship gatherings organized around those themes and responses will more naturally include pastoral prayers that apply God's promises to people's predicaments. Sermons with a repeated point of application or with an incisive rebuke of sin will shape the service in ways that encourage confession and repentance in believers. As worship planners thoughtfully reflect on the passage to be preached, a direction for prayer emphases usually becomes obvious.

The nature and extent of a congregation's needs should factor into the planning of prayer. A principle for individual prayer is helpful in conducting corporate prayer. Paul commands believers to put away anxiety and to put on prayer (Philippians 4:6). When anxiety triggers are pressing in on a congregation, church leaders should devote time in the public worship gathering to praying for these matters. Emergencies and tragedies at the individual, local, national, and global levels are all appropriate contexts for prayer. Praying through these difficulties will model for Christians the response God desires from his people. In the rare times that a church enjoys relative peace from trials, that church has the opportunity to focus its attention on the needs of other gospel-true churches, especially ones in areas hostile to the truth.

The frequency of prayer emphases is another premise for worship-planning decisions. Regularly worship planners should ask questions like, "When was the last time we had a prayer of confession?" Every element of the worship service is an instructional resource. Ministers are teaching their congregations what our worship of the true and living God really is. If the main prayer of every weekly gathering focuses entirely on intercession, the church is encouraging Christians to pray only for pressing needs. By varying the emphases of prayer on a consistent basis, the church guides Christians toward healthy private prayer lives.

Resources for Corporate Prayer

Worship planners should consult a few resources as they plan the direction of corporate prayers. The prayers dictated and depicted in the New Testament are a rich supply of ideas and inspiration. Ministers can glean many important lessons from the prayers, teachings on prayer, and requests for prayer of Jesus (Matthew 6:6–14; Luke 18:1–8; John 17), the apostles (Acts 4:23–31; 12:5; 14:23), and Paul (Ephesians 3:14–21; 6:18–19; Philippians 1:3–11; Colossians 1:9–14; 4:2; 2 Thessalonians 3:1–2; 1 Timothy 2:1–2). The content of these prayers gives Christians language to use and issues to focus on in their own prayers. Corporate prayer provides ministers an opportunity to model biblical faithfulness in prayer.

Record keeping will benefit worship planners. By tracking who prayed and what was prayed in services, church leaders can ensure a healthy variety of intercession, confession, petition, and praise in the church's prayer life. Variety, however, is not the main goal in coordinating the church's corporate prayer times. If a series of sermons consistently reflects on God's promises, or if a church endures a season of adversity, leaders should not hesitate to lead the congregation in ways that highlight the preaching of God's word and that serve believers' needs.

As with other areas of worship planning, consistency in personal spiritual disciplines often improves ministers' leadership in prayer. When a minister experiences fervency in praying for a matter, he will enthusiastically lead the church to pray for that issue. At our church, we noticed this phenomenon as the pastors prayed earnestly for a greater evangelistic impact in our neighborhood. The church willingly embraced this prayer emphasis. Our church not only is regularly praying for evangelistic opportunities and conversions but also is more actively participating in outreach efforts.

CHAPTER 6

PLANNING THE SINGING OF THE WORD

WORSHIP MUSIC HAS BECOME a key identifier for local churches. Descriptors like "contemporary," "traditional," "blended," and "arts" are often innuendos for music styles and song repertoires. However, the most important descriptions of worship, as argued in chapter 2, are ones like "congregational" and "corporate" that capture the New Testament's teaching on worship. The task of planning the worship songs for a weekly gathering is not about perpetuating perceptions about your church. Worship planners ought to equip believers to carry out the commands to edify one another through "psalms and hymns and spiritual songs" and to address their praises to God with a heartfelt melody (Ephesians 5:19 ESV).

Criteria for Planning Songs

Worship planners should apply several principles as they select and arrange songs for worship gatherings. We commend coherence with the content of the sermon as a high priority for worship planning. Since God's word is his means for making us wise, rebuking, correcting, training, completing, and equipping us (2 Timothy 3:14–17), the whole service should prepare believers to hear, accept, believe, love, submit to, and obey the Scriptures. Songs have a unique capacity for summarizing and reinforcing Christian instruction. Song choices can drown out the message of the sermon, or they can amplify the word-based charge for God's people.

We long for God's word to overwhelm us each Sunday, and we leverage every moment of the service toward that end. The process for choosing songs is similar to our process for choosing Scripture readings. We search for songs that address themes and for keywords related to the sermon passage and message. Our repertoire includes classic hymns, modern songs, and paraphrases of psalms set to familiar tunes. Our final choices relate in some way to the sermon; however, some relationships are more obvious than others. Often, a single line of hymn is so close to the anticipated direction of a sermon that we will choose it, even when the rest of the hymn is only loosely related to the sermon. Preferably, selected songs have multiple points of cohesion with the sermon.

Adherence to biblical doctrine is a mandatory prerequisite. No song that expressly violates a tenet of the Christian faith should receive an audience in the church. Relatively few hymns are forthright in rejecting biblical doctrine, but many introduce content that is vaguely in tension with Scripture. We have pared down our repertoire over the years by not selecting hymns that are too individualistic—such as "In the Garden," which describes an individual's communion with Christ as an experience "none other has ever known"—because we want to accentuate the congregational nature of Christian worship.

Planning the Singing of the Word

A conviction to articulate the gospel should inform the planning process. Each worship service should explicitly declare Jesus' accomplishment of salvation through his incarnation, death, and resurrection, as well as the believer's reception of salvation through faith and repentance. Make it a goal for at least one song in the service, but preferably many more, to spell out the details of the gospel. The confession of gospel truths is what the church is built on (Matthew 16:13–20), and so each week, the church should vocalize the core beliefs that define its existence. Few things encourage believers as much as hearing their brothers and sisters in Christ joyfully sing of their common redemption, and a loud, corporate exultation in Christ's person and power communicates the magnificence of the gospel to unbelievers.

Worship planners should prioritize the congregation's needs and interests (Philippians 2:3–4) in their planning practices. Churches exist in unique cultural and socioeconomic contexts. Congregations will vary in their intellectual and musical gifting, and this variation should impact the choice of songs. Planners should analyze the language of potential song choices and consider whether the song communicates effectively to a particular congregation. A doctrinally rich hymn may need to be neglected if it is chockablock with archaic words. Moreover, the complexity and range of a song's melody deserve scrutiny. Worship planners need to assess the congregation's singing abilities and plan songs that will encourage rather than frustrate God's people.

Accounting for the congregation's traditional hymnody is another necessary task for worship planners. Each service should feature a number of songs that are very familiar to the congregation. Christians' fond association with certain hymns and modern songs is an asset that ministers should employ in developing services that encourage congregations. The New Testament expects Christians to edify one another with their singing (Ephesians 5:19–21; Colossians 3:16–17). Yet, if the order of worship is replete with unusual words, uncomfortable melodies, and unrecognizable tunes, Christians will not effectively address one another in song. Rather, they will stumble and mumble through the singing.

On the other hand, new lyrics and new tunes can be good tools for church leaders, especially in filling thematic gaps in the church's worship repertoire. A wise way to balance these concerns is to introduce new songs at a slow pace. Before asking the congregation to sing the song, allow it to hear the song on several occasions by playing it before the service, performing it during the collection of the offering, and providing access to the song online and through social media. When introducing a new song, if it is possible and practical, sing the song congregationally for several consecutive weeks. This repetition will allow the church to familiarize itself with the song. In the order of worship, surround new songs with familiar ones; by doing so, believers who are less musically inclined will have an encouraging follow-up.

Song selection should account for the emotional responsiveness of the music. In chapter 3, we contended that worship should reflect the diverse emotions of biblical spirituality. If your church has experienced a tragedy, do not respond by planning a service that quickly lifts the spirits of the congregation. Acknowledge the emotional and spiritual condition of your congregation in your planning. Furthermore, intended emotional responses should play a role in planning. Sermons that push Christians toward confession and repentance deserve a worship service that encourages those same responses. More than likely, a service that begins with upbeat, celebratory tunes does not prepare Christians well for the introspection necessary for repentance.

Resources for Planning Songs

Worship planners have an abundance of resources for identifying and selecting worship songs. We want to share with you the resources that have been most helpful in our planning. In our ministry context, we have adopted what may be called a "blended" style of worship music. When Brian began pastoring our church over a decade ago, the congregation consisted primarily of later-in-life adults. In order to serve these faithful saints, we have retained their preferred hymnal and instrumentation, while patiently adding high-quality contemporary worship songs and some variation in accompaniment. Our readers who are in congregations with different musical emphases—arts-integrated, contemporary, expressionistic, jazz, Latino, or Southern gospel, to name only a few—can thoughtfully adapt many of these planning practices to their settings.

A congregation benefits from having one or two basic hymnals or songbooks. If your church is an established church and not a recently planted congregation, you likely have a hymnal or songbook that you inherited from previous generations. For instance, our church has used the 1991 edition of the *Baptist*

Hymnal, published by Lifeway Christian Resources, for many years. Even a hymnal of this size—over six hundred entries!—will have gaps in the doctrines and themes it addresses. A secondary hymnal will provide church leaders additional hymns that enrich the church's song rotation. The *Trinity Hymnal*, which is distributed by Great Commission Publications, has proven to be a valuable resource of doctrinally potent songs for our church.

One tool these hymnals offer is a topical index. After we have pinpointed the themes and keywords for our weekly worship planning, we often consult these indices for song suggestions. The *Baptist Hymnal* has entries for general topics such as "Cross" and "Resurrection." Unfortunately, more specific themes are not addressed in this hymnal's index. However, the *Trinity Hymnal* has one of the most comprehensive topical indexes we have seen. We are no longer surprised to find minute topical headings like "Omnipotence."

Of course, the association of hymns and topics in these indices is subjective. Some entries bear a strong thematic resemblance to their topics, while others have a less than clear relationship. Over time, worship planners can develop their own skills for thematic associations. The most helpful tools for planners, in this regard, are online searchable databases. Hymnary.org has become an indispensable resource for us. The site's search function allows us to identify hymns that contain keywords related to the expected content of the sermon. Users can include hymnal codes (e.g., "bh1991" for the *Baptist Hymnal* 1991) to find entries from their basic hymnals that have these keywords. For instance, a search for "bh1991 wisdom" yields sixteen results, including "My God, How Wonderful You Are," "Be Thou My Vision," "Ye Servants of God," and "Teach Me, O Lord." This search process has improved our ability to craft services that stay on topic, while also introducing us to a few unfamiliar hymns in our own hymnal.

A lesser-known resource for finding hymns is the index of tunes found in many hymnals. The melodies of everyone's most beloved hymns typically have a tune name that is often different than the hymn title. For example, the popular hymn "Amazing Grace" is set to a tune named "New Britain." Hymnals often reuse tunes by having several hymns with different words set to the same tune. The 1991 *Baptist Hymnal*, for instance, has three songs set to a tune known as "Azmon"; these songs include "My God, How Wonderful You Are," "O for a Thousand Tongues to Sing," and "The Love of Christ Who Died for Me." If your church is desperate for some new content in your worship songs, spend a couple of hours in your hymnal's index of tunes. Highlight any tune name that corresponds with multiple entries (e.g., Azmon 11, 216, 268). When you compile all the frequently used tunes, you will likely discover a number of new hymns. For finding even more hymns, compare the tune index of your primary hymnal (in our case, the 1991 *Baptist Hymnal*) with the tune index of your secondary hymnal (in our case, the *Trinity Hymnal*). We call these correlations of unfamiliar texts and familiar tunes "new songs/old tunes." These new songs/old tunes are easy to incorporate into services because the congregation already knows the melody. When we applied these processes to our hymnals, we found more than forty new songs, which we list in appendix 3.

Worship planners in other contexts may not have access to these resources. For instance, congregations that only incorporate contemporary worship music will likely use an eclectic repertoire instead of using one or two hymnals. In this case, worship planners should develop a unique index for their rotation of songs. Unleash your creativity on organizing your church's worship music. For each song, list two or three key themes. Consider a mix of theme descriptions that are theological (e.g., Trinity, gospel, conversion) and practical (e.g., evangelism, marriage, prayer). Appropriate emotional responses (e.g., joy, mourning, steadfastness) can be useful tags in arranging your selections. This exercise will prove immensely helpful for a theme-based approach to planning weekly services. In addition, this work will show gaps in the range of themes your church's songs address. A worthy long-term project for worship planners is to fill those gaps.

We wholeheartedly endorse the use of old, traditional hymns. Singing the hymns written centuries ago connects contemporary Christians with brothers and sisters from different points in history and different parts of the world. These hymns communicate the power of the gospel to transcend the constraints of time and place. However, we also endorse modern hymns. A number of gifted contemporary Christians are writing songs with elegant modern melodies and bold declarations of biblical truth and historic Christian belief. Finding these songwriters requires some effort because often they are not featured on contemporary Christian radio stations. Perhaps the most popular modern hymnists are Keith Getty and Stuart Townend. These believers have crafted many viable modern hymns, including some of our church's favorite songs, such as "In Christ Alone," "Speak, O Lord," "How Deep the Father's Love for Us," and "The Power of the Cross." Sovereign Grace Music, led by Bob Kauflin, has contributed several songs that our congregation loves as well: "All I Have Is Christ," "Before the Throne of God Above," "Behold Our God," and "To Live Is Christ." The ongoing Indelible Grace collaborative project introduced us to "Jesus, I Come" and "Thou Lovely Source of True Delight," and Indelible Grace's albums have many other good options. Sandra McCracken, who participates in Indelible Grace projects, is one of our favorite modern hymnists because of songs like "Thy Mercy, My God" and "In Feast or Fallow." Other modern hymn movement resources we admire include Sojourn Music, BiFrost Arts, and Matt Boswell. Any of these resources would be a good starting point for expanding your church's worship repertoire.

We are passionate about two other resources. First, our church has focused much effort and energy on psalm singing. As laid out in appendix 1, we believe the singing of psalms is faithful to the New Testament, follows the example of church history, leads believers to a greater confidence in God's word, and promotes a well-rounded biblical spirituality. Our method of psalm singing is to set paraphrases of psalms to familiar tunes. The *Trinity Psalter* is a great source for psalm paraphrases that adhere to metrical conventions of traditional hymnody. By setting these versions of the psalms to tunes of familiar hymns (e.g., "Come, Thou Fount of Every Blessing" or "O for a Thousand Tongues to Sing"), we have introduced psalm singing as a regular part of our worship experiences.

Appendix 2 includes five of the psalm arrangements we use most often.

Second, our church has produced a musical version of our church's covenant. We use a covenant as part of our membership and discipleship process. New members are expected to agree and adhere to our church's covenant. We regularly review the covenant in our teaching ministry, and we recite the covenant at each of our members' meetings (i.e., business meetings). This pledge makes clear the expectations of church membership to all of our members. The musical version of the church covenant can be found in appendix 4. It is a useful service element for important occasions, such as the Lord's Supper, or for sermons that focus on church unity.

Conclusion

Worship planners can use a variety of methods in their decision-making processes. These leaders can use their own personal preferences to lead the worship of the church, but the job of a shepherd is to tend to the needs of the sheep. Ministers can plan worship based on preconceived notions of trendiness, but a pastor should seek the approval of God, not of man. Church leaders can make worship decisions on the fly with no driving purpose and no rationale, but they of all people should know that God blesses and favors the diligent (Proverbs 10:4; 12:24, 27; 13:4; 21:5). If selfishness, fear of man, and haphazardness characterize your worship planning, put these things away, and dedicate your leadership in this area to planning services that admonish, edify, and instruct your fellow believers.

PART 3

LEAD WORSHIP

CHAPTER 7

LEADING READINGS AND PRAYERS

OUR CULTURE IS increasingly moving toward customization. Consumers are accustomed to personalizing their desserts at yogurt shops, inventing drinks at Coca-Cola Freestyle machines, attuning their musical tastes through streaming music services, and individualizing their online experience by following, Liking, and pinning. Corporate worship, however, calls Christians to an experience quite different from consumerism. Christians partake of five elements in corporate worship—preaching, praying, the reading of Scripture, singing, and the ordinances. This participation, however, is mediated through the church. The church's leaders, who are gifted by God and affirmed by their local congregation, arrange the elements of worship by developing detailed and explicit plans. Then these leaders administer the elements to Christians by preaching, reading Scripture aloud to the congregation, praying in the gathering, giving worship instructions, singing, conducting baptisms, and overseeing the Lord's Supper.

The congregation is both active and passive in worship. In one real sense, they actively participate in these elements as they offer praise and thanks to God. In another sense, they are receiving what has been prepared by the ministers for that particular week. Hence, ministers must prepare to present the various elements in the service in a way that aids the worship of the congregation rather than hinders it. Presentation is, therefore, no trivial matter. Those individuals tasked with worship leadership bear a great responsibility to shepherd God's people. This chapter provides practical guidance to ministers on leading worship. Our particular focus is on the administration of four worship elements: reading the word, praying the word, singing the word, and seeing the word.

Leading Readings

Christian worship must include the public reading of Scripture and corporate prayer. In the last chapter, we described the planning process we use for determining Scripture readings and a mid-service prayer focus. Since these elements have a biblical mandate and we expend much effort in planning these elements, we want to encourage God's people to receive these elements rightly. Our desire is for believers to hear his word, affirm it as true, and submit to its authority in their lives. Similarly, we want our congregation to join the corporate prayer time by lending the prayers of their hearts to the issues at hand. In our experience, quality leadership is a vital connecter between the planned elements and people's response.

For each corporate gathering, we designate a service leader. For the Sunday morning gathering, the service leader is usually one of our church's pastors (a role some churches assign to an elder). Whatever your church's polity, the service leader should be recognized as a leader in the mold of Hebrews 13. In that passage, Christians are admonished to "remember," "have confidence in," and "submit to" their leaders (Hebrews 13:7, 17). If the service leader is recognized in this way, he has the credibility to instruct the church toward meaningful worship activities, like confession of sin. In our worship gatherings, the service leader reads the call to worship, gives an opening prayer, reads a mid-service Scripture reading, leads the mid-service prayer, and concludes the service with prayer and the final benediction. His primary responsibilities, then, are leading readings and leading prayers.

The qualities necessary for leading Scripture readings are primarily intuitive. At a minimum, the service leader must read Scripture passages loudly, clearly, and slowly. Ability to project is a nonnegotiable at our church. Though we amplify everyone who speaks from the pulpit, projection is still important. Be especially mindful of the need to project one's voice in a congregation with elderly members. The gradual loss of hearing is frustrating to older members, and failing to project stokes their feelings of frustration and embarrassment, which prevents the emotional response intended in the planning process.

In order to achieve clarity in reading, the service leader needs to review all selected passages beforehand. He should make sure he has a sense of the flow of the sentences and that can pronounce all of the words in the passage. For those difficult Hebrew words, a good principle is that no syllable has more than one vowel (e.g., Zeruiah, 1 Kings 2:5, consists of four syllables, Ze-ru-i-ah), though anglicizing common Hebrew terms is appropriate (e.g., "Dan-yil" for Daniel, instead of Da-ni-el). The service leader must also give due regard to the pace of his reading. A frenetic pace will detract from the significance of the Scripture reading by either distracting the congregation or subtly communicating irreverence toward God's word. A few pacing techniques—such as maintaining a deliberate speed and pausing before or after key lines of text—appeal to the ear of the congregation and encourage engaged listening.

The service leader can enhance Scripture readings with short introductions. Call to worship introductions should be very short; in fact, "Our call to worship text this morning is ... Listen as I read" is sufficient. For a thematic mid-service Scripture reading, an introduction can give cues to the congregation on what to listen for in the passage. The use of imperatives—"as we read this passage, *pay attention to* ..."—will foster active listening on part of the congregation. The service leader can use introductory remarks to make explicit connections between the Scripture reading and the service: "Later this morning, Pastor Brian will exhort us to avoid idolatry, and here in our Scripture reading from Exodus 32 we see that God's people have always been prone to follow other gods."

Scripture reading introductions are useful in preparing God's people for specific actions. Before a prayer of confession, a service leader might introduce a Scripture reading by saying, "Our Scripture reading this morning is 1 John 2:1–6. In a few moments, we will confess our sins together. Let us do so remembering, as the apostle John writes, that when we sin, we have an advocate in Jesus Christ, God's Son." It is helpful to avoid bleeding over into exposition of a particular reading as it is introduced. A service leader can shift from leader to expositor rather quickly, which changes the purpose of that moment in the service. A Scripture reading needs to be chosen in such a way that enables it to be heard and understood in plain reading. Trust in the power and effectiveness of God's word simply being read and heard. Introduce the reading as such, knowing that explanation and exposition are soon to come.

The conclusion of a Scripture reading provides another opportunity for worship leadership. The service leader can conclude the Scripture reading in a way that conveys the significance of the word read aloud. Even a simple "Amen" confidently punctuates a Scripture reading. Some service leaders end their readings with the reminder that "this is the word of the Lord." Others use a statement like "blessed be the word of the Lord" to encourage the congregation in believing what it has heard. A brief conclusion that communicates convictions about Scripture and is consistent with the leader's personality supports the reading of God's word.

Leading Prayers

Many of the skills necessary for reading Scripture in a worship service are applicable for leading prayer. Clarity, projection, and speed are just as important in prayer. Unfortunately, many tend to pray aloud more quietly than when using a normal speaking voice. Perhaps they think a whisper befits the disposition and emotion of prayer. Yet, since Jesus stresses the power of agreement in Christian prayer (Matthew 18:19), those leading prayer in the public gathering should make every effort to be heard. The length of the prayer is no trivial matter either; service leaders should esteem the congregation more highly than themselves, prioritize issues, and reasonably limit the duration of the prayer.

Silence is one of the service leader's assets, not a liability, during times of prayer and throughout the rest of the service. An aptly timed pause in prayer—or even a pause between two service elements—can enrich the service in a couple of ways. Silence fosters introspection among the congregation. During prayers of confession, a moment of silence encourages believers to engage in their own personal confession. Prior to a closing prayer, silence provides an opportunity for the congregation to consider the whole service and its implications for their pursuit of Christ in the week ahead. Silence has a unique ability to connote weightiness. Using silence at the end of a pastoral prayer in which many difficult congregational needs have been prayed for draws out the importance of intercession and even aids Christians in mourning with those who mourn. Incorporating intentional times of quiet reflection is worth the attention and creative energy of worship planners.

In order to make a prayer as clear and accessible as possible, service leaders should engage in at least some preparation prior to the service. A degree of preparation will minimize the techniques (e.g., "um," "just," and repetition of phrases) often used to fill time as those who pray think of what to say next. Many leaders will approach prayer preparation differently. We have known some men who prepare word for word what they intend to pray. Others simply develop a list of requests and praises. Prior reflection on the sermon passage and selected Scripture readings is a good preparation for public prayer. Reading over these passages will bring to mind issues for corporate prayer. A service leader tasked with reciting the Lord's Prayer, for example, should consider including in a pastoral prayer intercession for physical needs, church unity, and victory over sin. When in doubt, pray God's word. Use the psalms not only as a model but as a source of content for public prayer.

The most helpful resources for ministers as they approach corporate prayer are already in their possession. Leading public prayer exposes us to a number of anxieties. Fearing that we will neglect a crucial matter, offend someone unintentionally, or speak incoherently are temptations that easily beset us. Yet, against these fears stands the "new covenant" reality of the Holy Spirit's abiding presence with us. The apostle Paul reminds us that "the Spirit helps us in our weakness," and though "we do not know what we ought to pray for," God's Spirit "intercedes for us" (Romans 8:26–27). We are inadequate for the task of leading a church in prayer, but since when does God accomplish anything through the adequacy of his people? Furthermore, those concerned with their rhetorical ineptness should remember that Jesus extols the virtues of determination, grit, and perseverance in prayer (Luke 18:1–8), not eloquence.

The Scriptures are inestimably useful in preparing for prayer leadership. As the service leader identifies areas of focus for corporate prayer, he should consult relevant passages of Scripture to shape the attitude and content of his prayer. The following issues are frequent, but not comprehensive, prayer concerns in our congregation that the Scriptures help us address. The one or more passages referenced for each issue are by no means exhaustive; however, from this sampling, worship planners and leaders will see how to infuse prayer with Scripture.

Members' Health Concerns. Second Corinthians 1:3–4 describes God as "the Father of compassion and the God of all comfort, who comforts us in all our troubles." As a service leader mentions specific members who have significant illnesses or injuries, he can theme his prayer around God's compassion and mercy, through which God would limit suffering, or around his comfort, in which God would sustain believers in the midst of suffering. The apostle John's prayer is another helpful model: "I pray that you may enjoy good health and that all may go well with you, even as your soul is getting along well" (3 John 2).

Expecting Mothers and Families with Newborns. Passages that depict God's providential care for humanity are appropriate reference points for prayer. Paul's address to a group of Greek citizens in Acts 17 gives theological reinforcement to an intercessory prayer for expanding families. A service leader could praise God, who "gives everyone life and breath and everything else" (verse 25), and then confidently intercede for healthy pregnancies, successful deliveries, and smooth transitions into parenthood.

Grieving Members. First Thessalonians 4 is often in our minds as we pray for those who have lost family members, friends, and other loved ones. Specifically, we pray that bereaved members would "not grieve like the rest of mankind, who have no hope" (1 Thessalonians 4:13). Another helpful passage for reflection is 2 Corinthians 1:3–4, as described earlier. The service leader should also remember Paul's instructions to "mourn with those who mourn" (Romans 12:15). Regularly, the church should pray for widows, who even many years after losing their spouses are painfully lamenting their loss. Remembering them in prayer is one way to fulfill the church's unique charge to care for widows (James 1:27).

Confession of Sin. Biblical models of repentance are great guides for leading corporate confessions of sin. Daniel's admission of guilt is well suited for corporate profession: "We have sinned and done wrong. We have been wicked and have rebelled" (Daniel 9:5). The prayers in Psalm 51—"Have mercy," "Wash away all my iniquity," "Cleanse me," and "Hide your face from my sins," among others—are appropriate pleas for forgiveness. Service leaders should consider New Testament texts that identify Christ as the source of forgiveness (e.g., Ephesians 1:7; Colossians 1:14; 1 John 1:8–9) and even quote portions of these texts in their prayers. Since there is "no condemnation for those who are in Christ Jesus" (Romans 8:1), Christians' confession of sin should always account for their redeemed state.

Legal Matters. Occasionally, the church will need to pray for favorable outcomes in matters decided by government officials, judges, and other authority figures. A church family pursuing the adoption of a child in another country may be facing excessive interference from foreign officials. A young mother whose husband has left her for an unstable and dangerous lifestyle has a petition before a judge to grant her full custody of her children. Passages that affirm God's sovereignty and prompt Christians' confidence in his rule bring hope to these uncertain situations. The prayer leader could intersperse his petition with declarations like "Our God is in heaven; he does whatever pleases him" (Psalm 115:3) or "In the Lord's hand the king's heart is a stream of water that he channels toward all who please him" (Proverbs 21:1).

A secondary source worthy of service leaders' attention is *The Valley of Vision*. This publication from Banner of Truth collects stately prayers from Christians of the past, especially the Puritans. The collection exemplifies doctrinally anchored, emotionally vibrant prayer. For praise-oriented opening prayers, sections like "Father, Son, and Holy Spirit," "Redemption and Reconciliation," "Approach to God," and "Gifts of Grace" include many prayers across a wide range of themes. Service leaders conducting pastoral prayers will find the "Needs and Devotion" section replete with candid expressions of dependence on and trust in God. "Penitence and Deprecation" provides examples of praying with keen awareness of the deceitfulness and sinfulness of the human heart. The concluding prayer of a worship gathering can draw from "Holy Aspirations" and "Service and Ministry" to consecrate the congregation to lives of obedience and sanctification. Ministers will find this resource useful in their private and public prayer lives.

Ministers should examine all aspects of their public prayer. Some aspects of our praying are so habitually engrained that they have lost their meaning. The vast majority of public prayers end with "in Jesus' name. Amen." This closing has biblical warrant (John 14:13–14) and deserves its prominent place in public prayer. A slight variation in the wording gives latitude for additional meaningful descriptions. The addition of a high Christological expression from Paul (Romans 9:5) makes the closing theologically ornate: "We pray in the name of Jesus, *who is God over all, forever praised! Amen.*" Service leaders could consider importing any of a number of similar biblical statements or other doctrinally rich formulations to enrich the closing of their prayers.

Conclusion

The role of service leader, which includes the responsibilities of reading Scripture and praying, requires faithful stewardship of authority and gifts. The church has several expectations for its service leaders. Thinking ahead, service leaders prepare by meditating on the sermon passage, familiarizing themselves with assigned readings, and carefully considering the circumstances and needs of the congregation. Speaking up, service leaders make sure the congregation can hear and recognize all that is said from the pulpit. Most importantly, service leaders convey the authority and sufficiency of God's word in the way they describe and read God's word and the way they rely on the Bible in their public prayers.

CHAPTER 8

LEADING SINGING

IN THE CURRENT CULTURE of evangelicalism, the phrase "leading worship" is most closely associated with leadership of worship music. This book argues for a more comprehensive understanding of worship leadership. Those who read Scripture, pray, and administer the ordinances are as involved in worship leadership as their musical counterparts. Many aspects of modern worship music leadership need reform. The basis of these reforms is the understanding of worship advocated throughout this book. Specifically, the congregational nature of singing calls for revised approaches to issues of leadership, amplification, and instrumentation.

Leader Approach

As with other elements of worship, congregational singing should be administered by a leader who is gifted by God and affirmed by the congregation. Affirmation as a pastor (or elder) or deacon would provide this leader with credibility to direct the congregation. At our church, we give this leader the responsibilities of introducing songs, giving instructions to the congregation, contributing to the vocals, and providing leadership to the accompanists. This work often involves giving spiritual commands. For instance, a leader will challenge Christians to examine their hearts for sin as a preparation for a corporate prayer of confession, or he will direct the congregation to praise, consider, or remember a particular biblical truth. Since issuing these commands constitutes a form of spiritual authority, we recommend that the designated leader—the key person who introduces songs and directs the congregation—should be male. This will safeguard churches' faithfulness to the Scripture's teaching on biblical manhood and womanhood, and in particular to the command of the apostle Paul for women not to "assume authority" over men (1 Timothy 2:12).

We understand that some readers disagree with our interpretation and practice in this area, and we recognize there are differences of opinion among scholars and church leaders on these issues. Regardless of the particular practice in your context, we challenge churches to carefully think through their views on authority and worship leadership and ensure that leadership in worship intentionally reflects their biblical convictions. Convenience and circumstance should never be the decisive criteria for decisions regarding worship leadership.

The specific criteria you determine may present barriers in some churches. The most musically gifted people in the church may not have an ordained leadership role, or the most passionate and talented vocalists in a congregation may be women. We are not saying that these able Christians should have no role in congregational singing! In fact, in our own church, we have accompanists and vocalists who assist in worship but do not lead or direct the congregation. Since the person who facilitates congregational singing will be giving a variety of directives to the entire church, if these instructions come from someone who is not biblically qualified or congregationally recognized, the effectiveness and enthusiasm of the congregational singing may well suffer.

Churches that think carefully about these criteria can usually overcome circumstantial or cultural barriers. An ordained leader, even one who is not particularly gifted as a musician, can introduce the songs and instruct the congregation. Then, for each song, the musicians can provide the accompaniment and vocals that facilitate congregational singing. If the leader is not singing or playing an instrument, he should still remain near the front of the congregation and serve as an example of enthusiastic participation in worship. Churches have flexibility and liberty as to how they practically account for the giftedness of their congregations and how they pursue faithfulness to the New Testament's pattern of church leadership. A leader who is ordained and affirmed by the church brings authority to worship leadership, and that authority will encourage the congregation's participation in the carefully planned worship service. In most cases, the accompanists and vocalists will appreciate the support of an ordained leader, since it removes one more thing from their often very stressful load.

Introducing Songs

Perhaps the most important responsibility in leading singing is introducing songs. Prior to each congregational song, the leader should give basic instructions. Clarity is fundamental for these introductions. The congregation needs to know what they are singing, where to find the lyrics, and how they should participate (e.g., sitting, standing). Leaders need the skill of artful repetition, in which basic facts are repeated, but not in a rote fashion. A bookend approach allows the leader to mention basic information (hymn number, song title, location of lyrics) twice: "Our next hymn is found in the *Baptist Hymnal*, number 147, 'And Can It Be.' Let's stand as we sing 'And Can It Be,' hymn 147." This form of introduction seemingly lacks sophistication, but many in the congregation—whether they have a hearing problem, are surrounded by chatty neighbors, or are distracted by an attention-seeking child—will miss this basic information if only stated once.

Song introduction can be a form of spiritual leadership. The leading singer can add to the basic instructions additional content that enriches congregational singing. The context for each song allows the leader to make connections among the worship elements. For instance, a connection between the opening Scripture reading (call to worship) and the first song makes for an effective song introduction. Here are a few examples of how these introductions function:

- "We have just heard the command from Psalm 100 to give thanks to our God and praise his name. Let's obey that command together as we sing our first song, hymn number 30 in the *Baptist Hymnal*, 'Stand Up and Bless the Lord.' Let's stand as we sing hymn 30, 'Stand Up and Bless the Lord.' "
- "In Psalm 73, the psalmist models what it looks like to desire God. Let it be our prayer this morning as we sing hymn 15, 'Come, Thou Fount,' that God would tune

our hearts to desire him. I invite you to stand as we sing hymn 15, 'Come, Thou Fount.' "

- "Let us now join the heavenly hosts of Revelation 5 in singing the praises of Jesus Christ, the Lamb of God. Our first song this morning is hymn 202, 'All Hail the Power of Jesus' Name.' Please stand as we sing hymn 202, 'All Hail the Power of Jesus' Name.' "

A short introduction can effectively unify the elements of the service. Frequently, a selected song foreshadows another element in the service. For example, a somber hymn like "Search Me, O God" encourages appropriate introspection among Christians prior to a corporate prayer of confession. A leader could introduce the hymn in this way: "In a few moments, we will corporately confess our sins. Let us prepare for that confession by singing hymn 297, 'Search Me, O God.' " When a hymn ties directly into an exhortation or a point of application in the sermon, the leader could use that connection to form the song introduction: "This morning, Pastor Brian will counsel us to consider our Christian brothers and sisters. Let's reflect on the unity of our church and prepare to hear the word preached as we sing hymn 382, 'God the Father of Your People.' " The song introduction allows the leader to make explicit connections among the service elements.

Notice that each of these examples is brief. The song introduction is not the music minister's equivalent to a sermon. Very rarely should a song introduction extend beyond a few sentences. In fact, segues between songs need little introduction beyond the basic details. When church leaders carefully plan the service, the selected songs integrate into the emotions and themes of the service. If a song needs an extended introduction to fit in a service, it is likely not an apt choice for that particular service.

Unfortunately, the song introduction is on its way out in many sectors of evangelicalism. Since many churches project lyrics onto screens—or at least try to—little need remains for basic instructions regarding song titles and locations. Some music ministries prefer a continuous stream of worship music that utilizes key changes to segue between songs. None of these trends are inherently wrong. Yet, the church that moves away from song introductions forfeits opportunities for leadership and instruction. A healthy approach would maintain these introductions, even as new technology is incorporated or as different approaches to instrumentation are utilized.

Amplification and Congregational Singing

If each member of a five-person praise band had the opportunity to adjust the soundboard, they would produce five different mixes of sound. Several of the members may want to increase the volume of their sound channel. Other members may seek to project their preferences across all channels; for instance, the bass player may detect too much treble in each channel. This experiment would yield a variety of results because the process of determining amplification is laden with subjectivity.

Not surprisingly, the Bible does not address how much gain to give the alto singer's microphone. Yet, the Scriptures give at least one principle that adds some objectivity to the process. The corporate worship that the New Testament envisions is congregational and corporate in nature. Recall that

Paul commands believers in Ephesus and Colossae to "address" and "admonish" one another with the singing of "psalms and hymns and spiritual songs" (Ephesians 5:19 ESV; Colossians 3:16 ESV). The common conception that worship has one audience is faulty; Christians sing to God *and* to each other.

An embarrassingly obvious implication of this principle is that Christians should be able to hear each other sing. Yet, in how many worship gatherings can an individual scarcely hear herself or anyone in close proximity sing aloud? Too many worship musicians have the fader pushed to eleven. Before anyone accuses us of prudishness, we admit we genuinely appreciate various genres of music, and each of us is in the rotation of instrumentalists at our church. We appreciate lead guitar parts, piano improvisations, chest-rumbling bass notes, and a thumping kick drum. Yet, in Christian worship all our preferences are subservient to God's precepts.

Amplification can support congregational singing in a few ways. First, the most important volume level is that of the vocalists. The congregation's primary need, when it comes to amplification, is hearing a lead vocalist who sings the melody for each song. The congregation follows this singer's lead on matters such as pitch, the beginning of verses, the duration of notes, and repetition of lines and words. Furthermore, by prioritizing the amplification of vocalists, the words of each song are clearer, and therefore the content becomes the distinguishing feature of each song. When there is male leadership in the introduction of songs, female vocalists can play a highly significant role in vocal leadership. In fact, some would argue that a woman's voice is the easiest for an entire congregation to follow.

This has rung true in our context. At the end of the day, *what* congregations sing is of greater importance than *how* they sing.

Second, members of the congregation should be able to hear each other. One of the most encouraging aspects of corporate worship is hearing the confident and joyous singing of other believers. What makes this experience special is not the terrific singing abilities of other believers. The context of *relationship* makes congregational singing meaningful. We hear believers who are suffering sing of the confidence, joy, hope, and trust they have in God. Their singing makes us realize again how mighty, gracious, merciful, and sovereign God is.

Third, the amplification of other instruments should only enhance these first two principles. A moderately amplified collection of a few instruments—piano, acoustic guitar, and bass guitar—along with lightly performed percussion, is helpful in establishing the key for congregational singing. Instrumentation can also help elicit the emotional response that worship planners intend for various song selections. The arrangements of songs and precise instrumentation can give song tones that are celebratory, peaceful, reflective, somber, or triumphant. Churches certainly have the freedom to decide on their instrumentation. Over the years, we have occasionally supplemented our core instruments with flute, trumpet, and mandolin. Yet, each congregation must ensure that instrumentation supports, not supplants, the purposes of worship.

Considering the Congregation

The one who leads the singing, along with the other vocalists and accompanists, must regard the gifts and needs of the congregation as they lead music. Of particular importance is the accessibility of the music. Some worship musicians forget that their singing ranges are more expansive than most people's ranges. While the temptation exists to select song keys that best accentuate the vocalists' ranges, the essential congregational nature of worship calls for reconsideration. Our experience is that songs with a high E note (E^5), which are often situated in the key of A, are too high for many men. If a church has musicians with adequate technical skills, songs set in high vocal registers should be transposed to lower keys. One way of obtaining music in a lower key is to look for the use of the tune for a different hymn; hymnals often set repeated tunes at different keys for this very purpose. Some online resources, such as Lifeway Worship, provide sheet music for hymns in multiple keys. Worship leaders receive a reward for this tedious work when they hear the congregation singing passionately, glorifying God as with one voice (Romans 15:6).

Consistency in musical arrangements is another way of respectfully leading the congregation. Accompanists and vocalists should strive to replicate the arrangements of songs each time they are used in the worship gathering. Our penchant for creativity works against this wise principle. Musicians may grow weary of playing hymns the same way each time and propose innovations like key changes or resetting music to a minor key. However, such significant changes often distract congregations. Complying with the congregation's expectations for a song encourages the assembly of believers to sing well.

The use of *a cappella*—the deliberate silencing of instruments to emphasize vocals—supports worship that is concentrated on the congregation. Hearing all the voices of the congregation maximizes the function of edification in corporate worship. Local church leaders should select a couple of stanzas from each worship service for an *a cappella* arrangement. A few options include stanzas that encapsulate key themes of the service, verses with moving expressions of gospel truths, and somber sections within songs that precede transitions to triumphant content. Songs selected for this special arrangement should be very familiar to the congregation and set to a comfortable key; otherwise, the use of *a cappella* is more discomforting than encouraging. The leading vocalists need to pay careful attention to preserving pitch and maintaining tempo, especially when *a cappella* is used in the middle of a song. One of our preferences is to select one or two stanzas in the whole service, rather than a stanza from each song, for this arrangement. This selectiveness preserves the capacity of *a cappella* to emphasize and highlight particularly noteworthy content.

On Special Music

The primacy of the congregation in worship does not preclude the occasional use of solos, duets, or other forms of "special music." When a small group of musicians lead a song, they are singing to the congregation in a way that reflects Paul's description of worship as "addressing one another" (Ephesians 5:19 ESV). Furthermore, the Scriptures contain scenes in which only a portion of the gathering of God's people sing (1 Chronicles 16:4–36; 2 Chronicles 5:11–13; 29:30). A song led and performed only by a few vocalists and accompanists can meaningfully and uniquely serve the congregation. However, recalling that Paul identifies "psalms and hymns and spiritual songs" as means for corporate encouragement should cause church leaders to scrutinize special music proposals thoroughly. Not everything useful for personal edification is well suited for the congregation. Only songs that cohere strongly with God's word are worthy of the congregation's silent contemplation.

In our church, we have used the time for collecting the offering as a strategic moment for congregation-edifying special music. Our regular pattern is for a couple of vocalists and accompanists to perform a portion of a psalm that is thematically aligned with the sermon and set to a familiar tune. This offertory music provides a moment of reflection for the congregation and prepares believers to hear the preaching of God's word. Furthermore, the practice does not subject Christians to doctrinally weak music that characterizes special music performances in many churches. We believe the Bible demands Christians' attention, and an offertory psalm is one way of communicating that belief to our church.

Another occasional use of special music is to introduce new "hymns and spiritual songs" to our congregation. We gradually introduce new music to our congregation and err on the side of overexposure. For example, if we plan to sing a new song congregationally at the end of a month, we will sing a stanza of that song as the offertory music for several weeks leading up to its congregational debut. Over the course of several weeks, the congregation becomes familiar with the tune and considers the content of the new song. This approach helps build awareness and anticipation for new songs that will encourage the church.

Conclusion

Many of our proposals for leading congregational singing react to perceived problems in evangelicals' worship. Congregational worship gatherings have been tragically overindividualized and trivially retrofitted for entertainment. Our desire is for Paul's instructions for a congregation-centric worship to topple the idolatry of self that is rampant in many churches. The role of those leading the singing of the word is to facilitate Christians' participation in a worship gathering that seeks the glory of God and the good of other believers. Local church leaders must reexamine their worship practices to ensure that the right priorities are guiding the weekly worship gatherings of the church.

CHAPTER 9

LEADING THE ORDINANCES

OF THE ISSUES DISCUSSED IN THIS BOOK, the ordinances are perhaps the most divisive. Different views on baptism and the Lord's Supper have balkanized Protestant Christianity. We have friends who disagree with our particular beliefs regarding these divinely instituted church practices, and we object to their vision for these ordinances as well. Obviously, this small book will not settle these centuries-long disagreements. Even in this divisive context, gospel-embracing believers share many like-minded views on the ordinances and their roles in Christian worship. This chapter seeks to give advice to ministers, even those whose views contrast with our own, on leading the ordinances.

Leader Approach

Christians often describe participation in the ordinances as "partaking." This language is helpful in articulating the role of ministers in the ordinances. The concept of service coheres well with the language of "partaking." Christians do not baptize themselves; rather, the act of baptism implies a close relationship between the one baptized and the one who conducts the baptism (1 Corinthians 1:14–16). A consistent pattern in Scripture—from Jesus' unique baptism to the baptisms conducted by the apostles—is for one person who has a recognized authority to administer baptism. The Lord's Supper has similar aspects of authority and reception. In Jesus' institution of this ordinance, he is a leader who instructs the participants and distributes the elements. Maintaining continuity with this example can help churches avoid the selfish and excessive abuses of the ordinance that occurred in the Corinthian church (1 Corinthians 11:17–34).

In light of these patterns, we propose that churches designate leaders of the ordinances. Because of the significance of the ordinances and their inherent reliance on authority, gospel ministers—those gifted by God and affirmed by the church for the ministry of the word—should conduct the ordinances. Administering these elements of Christian worship is undeniably an act of spiritual leadership. During the Lord's Supper, a leader often commands the members of a congregation to examine themselves. At a new believer's baptism, a leader will often ask the recipient to pledge to follow Christ. These types of directives are most appropriately given by the ones whom the local church has invested with the unique authority of the pastoral office.

The Practicalities of the Ordinances

Each church needs to have a clearly articulated understanding of the ordinances from which the church's leaders can draw to make decisions on practical issues pertaining to these elements. A church's statement of faith should include a section on the ordinances. The document should define the ordinances, set forth their purposes, and regulate who may participate in the ordinances. Our church's statement of faith is the Abstract of Principles, which was developed for The Southern Baptist Theological Seminary at its founding in the 1850s. The key features of this statement's teaching on the ordinances limit baptism to believers, require believers' baptism as a prerequisite for church membership and participation in the Lord's Supper, and distinguish our view of the Lord's Supper from the transubstantiation view of Catholicism.

The church's ordained leadership should agree on a few practical issues. The frequency of the ordinances is one such matter. As churches see conversions in their communities, they will need to decide on the frequency of baptisms. Some churches address this issue by having quarterly baptismal services. However convenient and expedient this method is, it is sometimes a flawed approach. For instance, Jason was baptized in a church that used this schedule, and the pastor mistook the next baptismal candidate for Jason's brother. Before the whole congregation, he announced, "Now, sit here while I baptize your brother." When Jason corrected him, he joked, "Well, he's your brother now!" As a contrast to this method, we have enjoyed integrating baptisms into the regular worship gatherings of our church and recommend this approach to other churches.

When it comes to the Lord's Supper, the New Testament depicts this ordinance as a regular activity of the church (1 Corinthians 11:20). We are sympathetic with the view that the church should celebrate the ordinance at its main gathering each week. However, we are ministering in a context with a tradition of infrequent participation in the ordinance. We have moved toward a minimum of participating in the Lord's Supper monthly, and when the sermons relate clearly to the ordinance, we administer it more often. Anything less frequent seems to contradict the pattern of Scriptures.

Some Christians view Paul's rebuke of the Corinthians (1 Corinthians 11:17–34) as a disincentive for frequent observation of the ordinance. Paul connects some believers' experiences of God's discipline through illness to their abuse of the Lord's Supper (1 Corinthians 11:30). A misinterpretation of the text is that believers must be free from the presence of sin in order to eat and drink worthily at the Lord's Table. However, Paul has a very specific abuse in mind, namely, that of disunity among Christians. We do not believe Paul is discouraging participation in the Supper; instead, he is discouraging division among Christians. The right response is not to abstain from the ordinance or only administer it on rare occasions. The right response is to repent of our failure to love other Christians as we should.

A highly practical issue is the order of worship elements when the ordinances are administered. We confess that we are a time-sensitive church, and we believe most congregations should be mindful of their starting and ending times. Therefore, when we celebrate the ordinances, we usually have one less song and prayer in our service. We are not keen on shortening the sermon for these occasions because often the one preaching needs additional time to connect his content to the ordinances.

Typically, baptisms at our church occur early in the service, after the call to worship and a couple of songs and before a Scripture reading, song, and offertory. This timing allows the minister and participant plenty of time to prepare for the baptism, as well as sufficient time to be ready for the sermon. Yet we have also observed that a baptism toward the end of the service after the sermon can be a helpful placement for this ordinance. It allows the gospel to be sung, heard, preached, and then seen in this visible representation. Regardless of its placement, incorporating the baptism within the service has aided our worship planning and allowed us to bring in unique content that supports our congregation's understanding of the ordinance and encourages them with its gospel significance.

For the Lord's Supper, our pattern is to receive the elements near the end of the service—after the sermon and before the closing hymn, final prayer, and benediction. This timing does not relegate the ordinance to being a footnote to worship. Rather, this pattern causes the service to culminate dramatically in the Lord's Supper.

Introducing the Ordinances

The church's leaders have a responsibility to prepare God's people for the ordinances. The congregation should know in advance that a service will include the ordinances. For baptism, this awareness allows the congregation to pray for and encourage those who are to be baptized. For the Lord's Supper, the advanced notice gives believers the opportunity to examine themselves and their relationships with other church members in anticipation of Communion.

The service should include introductions to the ordinances. Through these introductions, ministers lead their congregations to engage and participate meaningfully in the ordinances. For baptisms, we introduce the ordinance at the beginning of the service. During our announcements, a pastor brings forward a candidate for baptism and asks the candidate to share their testimony to the whole congregation. On certain occasions, a pastor will read the testimony for candidates; however, we strongly encourage candidates to do this for themselves. Prior to the baptism, an appropriately themed Scripture reading (e.g., Romans 6) or hymn ("Jesus, Our Lord and King") prepares the congregation to see this visible representation of conversion. When the minister and candidate enter the baptistery, a few short remarks that remind the church of its views on baptism are helpful. Pastors need to teach about baptism regularly so that introductions to this ordinance are reminders of what the congregation already knows.

The Lord's Supper requires a bit more of an introduction. The minister leading this ordinance needs to explain the meaning of the elements. Most importantly, the introduction should explicitly detail the gospel truths of Jesus' death and resurrection. Believers will receive encouragement as they consider how Jesus accomplished their redemption. Unbelievers will see a picture of how Jesus gave up his body and poured out his blood for the remission of sins. Another important aspect of introducing the Lord's Supper is what some call "fencing" the table. The minister who presides over the Lord's Supper is entrusted with the task of sustaining the church's ordinances.

This responsibility entails setting clear boundaries for who can participate in the Lord's Supper. Our church takes its cues from the book of Acts, which has a pattern of unbelievers' experiencing conversion, undergoing baptism, becoming a part of the church, and then breaking bread with believers (Acts 2:41–42). We lovingly ask unbelievers to refrain from the elements, and we encourage them to consider the gospel that this ordinance displays. In addition, we ask visiting Christians who have not been baptized as believers to serve our church graciously in maintaining biblical faithfulness to this pattern by not receiving the elements. At that point, the decision to participate in the ordinances is left to the conscience of those in attendance. How your church articulates its understanding of the Lord's Supper should inform how your ministers lead this ordinance.

Conclusion

Christians who disagree on some of the finer points of the ordinances still share a great unity in the gospel of the Lord Jesus. Though we may differ on the participants, frequency, and even modes of these ordinances, we all know that the ordinances are an important part of the corporate worship and witness of the church. Gospel ministers must lead the ordinances in ways that accentuate the gospel for the purposes of edifying believers and warning unbelievers. Our desire is that ministers will give deliberate attention to how they lead these ordinances. Set aside time in your worship planning to consider how you will craft services that promote these grace-sharing means. Make sure you regularly instruct the congregation on these ordinances. In anticipation of administering these ordinances, think carefully how you will introduce them. Attention to these details will improve your leadership and your church's experience of the ordinances.

THE NEXT STEPS

OUR PRAYER IS THAT this little book has sharpened your understanding of Christian worship, enriched your ability to plan worship gatherings, and impressed on you the necessity of shepherding God's people through corporate worship with strong leadership. We wrote *Gather God's People* in the hope that young ministers would have a useful resource as they enter pastoral ministry. We also anticipated that some concepts would challenge experienced worship planners and leaders. If we have accomplished our goals, you likely have at least a few ideas to try out at your church. Three final admonishments will serve you well as you consider the application of this book.

Exercise Patience

If you implement this book's recommendations next Sunday, you are setting up your church for conflict and division. Please don't haul your lead guitarist's amp to the trash! Very few necessary changes in the church require immediate action. Only matters that compromise the gospel must be dealt with quickly. The best way you can serve your church as you seek biblical faithfulness in its weekly gatherings is to teach through the Bible's instructions for worship. Make it a high priority to exposit from the pulpit Paul's worship instructions to the

Ephesians (5:19–21) and the Colossians (3:16). Perhaps read this book—or very useful works like *The Deliberate Church* and *Give Praise to God*—with small groups of influential leaders in your church.[4] Assess the musicians' willingness to follow your leadership in these matters. Start with a few small goals, and then pray and persevere until you see them accomplished. No church has achieved pure biblical fidelity, and you should be content with whatever pace of progress best serves those in your charge.

Bear with One Another

We have discouraged you from directing the worship of your church based on your whims. A danger is that you will merely use this book to acquire new preferences and then unwisely force those preferences on your church. For example, we have commended psalm singing throughout this book and in appendix 1. Interestingly, we have been critiqued for not singing psalms exclusively. Do not make the mistake of preoccupying yourself with one aspect of Christian worship to the neglect of others. When you eventually implement something new, like psalm singing, integrate it into your existing worship repertoire.

Certain songs are beloved by your congregation, and that affection is primarily a good thing. Continue to choose service elements that your church enjoys. Only eliminate what is clearly unhelpful and obviously unbiblical. By maintaining what your church is fond of, you esteem them more highly than yourself, bear with them in love, and prioritize their encouragement above your own.

Remember What's at Stake

We end this book where we started. God desires and seeks his own glory in all things, including in the worship of the church. The task before you is first and foremost for God's glory. Over the long term, as you encourage your church's desire for biblically faithful worship, you are not seeking glory for yourself or a good reputation for your church. What magnifies him most is to rely on the means he has ordained for his glory. By following Scripture's examples and obeying its commands, you give each member of your church the opportunity to make this purpose their own: "In the assembly I will praise you" (Psalm 22:22). May the worship of all the congregations of the body of Christ resound to his glory and honor forever! Amen.

APPENDIX 1

REINTRODUCING PSALM SINGING

IN 1815, EIGHTY PROTESTANT CHRISTIANS in Nismes, France, experienced persecution at the hands of an anti-Protestant mob.[5] Many of these believers were beaten and dragged through the streets. Moments before the onslaught of violence, even as the mob was trying to force open the doors of the church, the ministers at Nismes sought to comfort the believers. They sang what could have been their last song this side of eternity—Psalm 42:

> Why are you cast down, O my soul,
> and why are you in turmoil within me?
> Hope in God; for I shall again praise him,
> my salvation and my God.

Perhaps that seems like an odd response to the threat of persecution. Yet, until quite recently, the psalms have provided the script for Christian devotion. For hundreds of years, the book of Psalms served as the hymnal and prayer book of Christians. To express joy and to describe grief, believers of many generations consistently turned to the 150 poems of praise collected at the center of their Bibles.

As an introduction to the idea of psalm singing, reflect on these words from the apostle Paul: "Be filled with the Spirit, addressing one another in psalms and hymns and spiritual songs, singing and making melody to the Lord with your heart" (Ephesians 5:18–19 ESV).

Paul's instruction in Ephesians 5 is his elaboration on the Lord's will. Instead of being controlled by substances (verse 18), Christians ought to live being filled with the Spirit. During corporate worship, Spirit-filled living manifests itself in joyful praise to God ("singing and making melody to the Lord with your heart").

However, Paul does not intend for congregational singing to be directed heavenward only. Even as we sing "up," we are also called to sing "out." Christian worship includes an element of encouragement and edification by which we address one another in "psalms and hymns and spiritual songs."

I will marshal Ephesians 5 later to support biblically the singing of the psalms, but, for now, I'll underscore that Paul envisions psalm singing as a means by which we encourage other believers. The Protestant persecution at Nismes, France, is a good example of how the psalms can strengthen us in life's situations.

As a more recent example of the sufficiency of the psalms, Terry L. Johnson, senior pastor of Independent Presbyterian Church in Savannah, Georgia, recounts a special psalm-singing service his church conducted in the wake of the September 11, 2001, tragedies.[6]

The congregation sang songs of grief, including Psalm 130:1–2, 5–6; 13:1–6; 25:16–20; and 142:1–6. What an appropriate time to sing, "Relieve the troubles of my heart and free me from my anguish" (Psalm 25:17)!

The congregation sang songs that implored God for his protection and justice, including Psalm 54:1–7; 57:1–5; and 71:1–6. Have we comfortable and safe evangelicals ever had a better occasion to sing, "Arrogant foes are attacking me; ruthless people are trying to kill me—people without regard for God" (Psalm 54:3)?

The congregation declared its trust in God through Psalm 23; 37:1–2, 10–19; 46:1–3, 10–11; and 91:1–12. Those God-inspired words "Be still, and know that I am God; I will be exalted among the nations, I will be exalted in the earth" vividly remind us of God's authority and power, even in the midst of tragedy.

The Rhyme and Reason of Psalm Singing

The argument for psalm singing is subtle and simple. Several straightforward principles should impress on us the necessity of psalm singing in the life of the church.

1. Psalm Singing Is Commanded.

In Ephesians 5, the apostle Paul elaborates on God's will for Christians. Characteristic of their Spirit-filled lives is that Christians address one another in "psalms and hymns and spiritual songs" (verse 19 ESV). In his letter to the Colossians, Paul includes this command in his description of Christians' new identity: "Let the word of Christ dwell in you richly, teaching and admonishing one another in all wisdom, singing psalms and hymns and spiritual songs, with thankfulness in your hearts to God" (3:16 ESV). And so we have two instances in which the apostle Paul instructs us to use the psalms in Christian worship.

Exegetical disclaimer: "Psalms" had a very broad use in the Greco-Roman world and often referred to religious music generally rather than the Old Testament psalms specifically. It is likely that Paul intends the Old Testament psalms, but would the Gentile audiences of Ephesians and Colossians have understood the term in this way?

There's evidence that early Christians understood Paul to mean the Old Testament psalms. Tertullian, Eusebius of Caesarea, Athanasius, Augustine, Jerome, and Sidonius Apollinaris are early church figures who refer to the practice of Old Testament psalm singing.

We should be careful to note that Paul does not impose on Christians the command to sing psalms *exclusively*. His reference to "hymns and spiritual songs" legitimizes other musical expressions of the church's doctrine. Paul obeyed his own command to make use of "hymns and spiritual songs." In a few instances, Paul cites early Christian poetry — perhaps, the vestiges of early Christian hymnody — in his teaching (Philippians 2:5 – 11; 2 Timothy 2:11 – 13). To demand that *only* Old Testament psalms be sung in the gathering of the church is a misconstrual of Paul's words in Ephesians 5 and Colossians 3.

2. Psalm Singing Is Significant.

Calvin aptly noted of the psalms, "When we sing them, we are certain that God puts in our mouths these, as if he himself were singing in us to exalt his glory."[7] We miss that certainty in many of the songs that fill our hymnals and populate our PowerPoints.

In my current ministry role, I'm active in planning worship services and selecting songs. I'm prone to dismiss certain songs for various reasons. For example, I might consider a tune to be hokey. Our *Baptist Hymnal* is fond of chord progressions full of seventh chords, which is good for toe tapping but sometimes feels dated.

Other times, I find some lyrics in a song to be unhelpful. I generally like the hymn "Word of God, Across the Ages" (*Baptist Hymnal* 1991, #262), except for the line that reads, "as devout and patient scholars more and more its depths reveal." I would not call the line unbiblical or erroneous, but I find it unhelpful. By God's Spirit, Christians can grow in their understanding of Scripture; they do not have to wait for an exegetical decree from a terminally degreed professor.

These concerns dissipate in psalm singing. If we truly believe that all Scripture is inspired, sufficient, and useful, the hokiest of tunes can be overcome. It takes a measure of irreverence to sing a God-inspired psalm and then critique the tune. Even more so, we will not find ourselves questioning the utility of the psalm's content.

When we sing the psalms, we sing words that are inspired (2 Timothy 3:16) and infallible and without flaw (Proverbs 30:5); we sing lyrics marked by permanence (Psalm 119:89; Isaiah 40:8) and power (Psalms 29:4; 33:6). These characteristics grant our worship a genuine significance, which no chord progression, key change, or guitar solo is able to invoke.

3. Psalm Singing Is Beneficial.

Put simply, singing the psalms benefits and edifies the church. Paul's instructions in Ephesians 5 and Colossians 3 presuppose that the psalms have value for admonishing and edifying Christians. Paul's presupposition is entirely correct: God's word is precious (Psalm 19:10), useful (2 Timothy 3:16), and the source of faith (Romans 10:17).

A unique benefit of the psalms is their articulation and expression of the range of human emotions. Of our modern praise choruses, which have the boldness to declare to God, "Why, LORD, do you reject me and hide your face from me?" (Psalm 88:14)?

Which of our modern praise choruses have the passion to declare to God, "Whom have I in heaven but you? And earth has nothing I desire besides you. My flesh and my heart may fail, but God is the strength of my heart and my portion forever" (Psalm 73:25–26)?

In March 2011, my father passed away. He languished in the hospital for several weeks. I found in the collection of psalms an unswerving support. They made me ever mindful of God's steadfast, unfailing love:

- "Show me the wonders of your great love" (17:7).
- "The LORD's unfailing love surrounds the one who trusts in him" (32:10).
- "May your unfailing love be with us, LORD, even as we put our hope in you" (33:22).
- "God sends forth his love and his faithfulness" (57:3).
- "Praise be to God, who has not ... withheld his love from me!" (66:20).

This is an example of the power of the psalms. Whether we "rejoice with those who rejoice" or "mourn with those who mourn" (Romans 12:15), the psalms give us the emotive language to edify one another.

The Practicalities of Psalmody

The issue of psalm singing serves as a crucible in which our belief in the authority, power, and sufficiency of Scripture is tested. How can those involved in leading the worship of the church reject psalm singing if they believe in the usefulness of Scripture and if they see the command, significance, and benefit with regard to singing the psalms?

The practicalities of psalmody can erect a barrier to the (re)inclusion of the psalms in corporate worship. Depending on your denominational affiliation, you may have never sung psalms and don't know where to find musical versions of the psalms.

To overcome these barriers, I will highlight some resources for psalm singing, provide guidance for (re)introducing the psalms melodically to your church, and address two lingering concerns. The relevance of the guidance will vary slightly in accordance with your church's unique worship setting.

Resources

For those in a "traditional" worship setting in which printed hymnals are still in use, you may be surprised to find in your hymnal some psalms set to music. "All People That on Earth Do Dwell" is a paraphrase of Psalm 100; most people will recognize the tune from "Praise God, from Whom All Blessings Flow." Hymnary.org lists twenty-five different hymnals that incorporate this psalm, including the 1991 and 2008 versions of the *Baptist Hymnal*. Isaac Watts's paraphrase of Psalm 23—"My Shepherd Will Supply My Need"—is another commonly published psalm.

Your church will likely need to look beyond the resources of its own hymnal. Two essential resources for psalm singing are the *Trinity Hymnal* and the *Trinity Psalter*. The *Trinity Hymnal* incorporates many psalms set to tunes with which your church may be familiar. I compiled a list of such psalms for my church.

Psalm	***Trinity Hymnal*** **Number/Title**	**Tune in *Baptist Hymnal* (1991)**
16:1–11	692: "To You, O Lord, I Fly"	339: "Not What My Hands Have Done"
25:1–10	694: "Lord, I Lift My Soul to Thee"	306: "Depth of Mercy"
45:1–10	169: "My Heart Does Overflow"	339: "Not What My Hands Have Done"
50:1–6	316: "The Mighty God, the Lord"	161: "Crown Him with Many Crowns"
69:16–36	607: "Thy Lovingkindness, Lord, Is Good and Free"	297: "Search Me, O God"
93	70: "With Glory Clad, with Strength Arrayed"	574: "Soldiers of Christ, in Truth Arrayed"
98	16: "Come, Let Us Sing unto the Lord"	587: "Jesus Shall Reign"
119:89–96	59: "Forever Settled in the Heavens"	587: "Jesus Shall Reign"

The *Trinity Psalter* has metrically arranged versions of all 150 Psalms. For each psalm, the Psalter lists a common tune to which the psalm can be sung. I found thirty-three psalms set to tunes familiar to my congregation. The only drawback to the *Trinity Psalter* is that it does not provide the musical score for the psalm. I address this issue by scanning the score of the tune and editing the psalm's text into the scanned image, which is time-consuming but rewarding. You can also consider purchasing the piano accompanist edition of the *Trinity Psalter*. To get you started in the right direction, appendix 2 contains five of the psalms we use most often.

Guidance for (Re)Introducing the Psalms

Consider these four principles for helping your congregation embrace the command, significance, and benefit with regard to singing the psalms.

1. Exercise patience in (re)introducing psalm singing. Young ministers sometimes struggle with patience in their first pastorate. We enter pastorates with a laundry list of reforms, which we too often rush to implement. Do not move psalm singing to the top of your reform list and fill next Sunday's order of worship with unfamiliar psalms. Apply Paul's instructions to bear with one another in love (Ephesians 4:2) and to "value others above yourselves" (Philippians 2:3), as you make your plans to incorporate psalms in worship. Remember that Paul valued "hymns and spiritual songs," alongside the psalms and therefore continue to sing the songs your congregation cherishes.

2. Cast a vision for psalm singing. Instruct your church about the value of singing the psalms. Exposit texts like Ephesians 5:17–21 and Colossians 3:12–17. In a Sunday school lesson or in the public preaching ministry, provide your people with a conceptual framework for psalm singing. Show them that singing psalms is an application of their beliefs about the perfection and profitability of God's word. If members of our churches share this vision, they will follow us more willingly as we lead them in psalm singing.

3. Expose your church to the musical psalms. Find a practical way to introduce a couple of psalms to your church. For instance, if your church services include "special music" or an offertory song performed as the offering is collected, sing psalms during that time. (By the way, this is a way of obeying Ephesians 5:19 and Colossians 3:16!) A vocalist or instrumentalist should alert the congregation that the song is a psalm. Ideally, the church will provide attendees a score of the psalm (in the bulletin or in a binder in the pew rack) so they can follow along as the psalm is performed. Follow up this exposure by singing the psalm congregationally in the not-too-distant future.

4. Alert the congregation to psalms in the order of worship. Whoever is responsible for introducing songs should make sure the congregation knows when psalms are sung. Tell the congregation that the song they are about to sing is a paraphrase of, for example, Psalm 23. Another helpful method is to read a psalm as a call to worship at the beginning of the church service (e.g., Psalm 100) and then sing the psalm (e.g., "All People That on Earth Do Dwell," #5 in the *Baptist Hymnal* 1991). Here is a sample song introduction in this scenario: "Let's sing back to God the words we have just heard from him in Psalm 100. Our first hymn is hymn 5, 'All People That on Earth Do Dwell,' which is a paraphrase of Psalm 100."

Two Lingering Concerns

Perhaps more than practicalities are inhibiting you from incorporating the psalms into the worship of your church. I want to address a couple of other potential concerns.

1. The musical psalms available are paraphrases of the psalms. Doesn't that negate some of the benefit of psalm singing?

Almost all musical versions of the psalms require some paraphrasing. The Old Testament psalms reflect conventions of Hebrew poetic meter and hymnody that do not translate easily to Western musical norms. Paraphrasing makes it possible to sing the content of the psalms in our modern context.

The utility of paraphrasing has some biblical endorsement. Second Samuel 22 and Psalm 18 contain substantially the same song of praise. However, when the two texts are collated and compared, over 100 variations exist between the two texts. An analysis of the two texts shows that 2 Samuel 22 transmits an older version of the song, and the variations that show up in Psalm 18—many of which have a devotional tone—are due to the liturgical use of the song in Israel's worship. Both 2 Samuel 22 and Psalm 18 are included in the corpus of Scripture; both are recognized as inspired and infallible. We can conclude, then, that we should not disqualify paraphrases, per se.

Do take care, however, to examine the paraphrased psalms before promoting them as psalms. For example, "Christ Shall Have Dominion" (#439 in the *Trinity Hymnal*) is listed as a paraphrase of Psalm 72:8–19. However, Psalm 72 has no occurrences of the word *Christ*. Perhaps we should be careful to refrain from calling this song a psalm. Those are the kinds of decisions each church and its worship planners should make.

2. The format of our church's worship is best described as contemporary. We sing mostly modern hymns and rarely incorporate older hymns. Most of our attendees are not familiar with older melodies and tunes.

This common scenario calls for an abundance of patience and wisdom as musical psalms are incorporated. Do the necessary preparatory work. Teach about worship, generally, and about psalm singing, specifically. Point church members to the rich historical tradition of psalm singing. Perform a psalm for the congregation before asking them to sing that psalm congregationally. You may need to incorporate musical psalms gradually and only occasionally.

However, you cannot use a contemporary orientation as an excuse to avoid psalm singing altogether. If you do so, you are essentially excusing yourself from obeying Paul's admonishments in Ephesians 5:19 and Colossians 3:16. Sadly, you are robbing your church members of the benefit and significance of psalm singing. Have you done them this disservice only because you lacked the courage to lead them?

Now Let's Sing

My aim—perhaps too ambitious—is to promote the recovery of psalm singing in modern evangelical churches. The discussion of the command, significance, and benefit with regard to psalm singing can provide the paradigm needed for (re)including the psalms in corporate worship. This appendix provides resources and guidance to get started. But the work is far from over. Together, let us strive to apply our convictions regarding the sufficiency of Scripture to our congregational worship.

APPENDIX 2

PSALMS SET TO FAMILIAR TUNES

THE FOLLOWING PIECES OF MUSIC are paraphrases of psalms set to familiar tunes.* These five psalms are ones we most commonly sing at our church congregationally and as special music. For each of these psalms, we specify a reasonably well-known hymn to describe the tune and cite entries in the 1991 *Baptist Hymnal* for reference. Accompanists can use their existing resources for performing these tunes, while vocalists and congregations use these inserts to sing the psalms. In addition, we have listed general themes that will be helpful for worship planning.

*All lyrics for the psalms in this appendix are taken from *Trinity Psalter*. Copyright © 1994 by Crown & Covenant Publications. Used by permission.

Psalms Set to Familiar Tunes

Psalm 16

Set to the tune of "Not What My Hands Have Done" (*BH*, 1991, #339). Themes: Eternal Life, Idolatry

1 Pre - serve me O my God; I put my trust in You
2 Their sor - rows mul - ti - ply Who af - ter i - dols seek.
3 The lines that fell to me En - close a plea-sant site
4 I al - ways keep the Lord Be - fore me, Him to see
5 My soul You will not leave In death's dark pit to be.

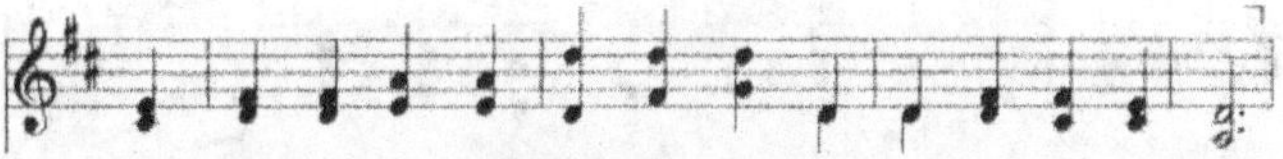

Lord, I con-fess, You are my Lord; No good have I but You
To them I'll no blood off'-rings make; Their names I'll ne - ver speak
The her - i - tage that I re-ceived To me is a de - light
Be - cause He is at my right hand I ne -vermoved shall be
Cor - rup -tion You will not per - mit Your ho - ly one to see.

The god - ly ones on earth, Those ho - ly in your sight
The Lord the por - tion is of my in - her - i - tance
I bless the Lord Who guides with coun - sel that is right.
Thus glad - ness fills my soul; My joy must be ex - pressed
The path of life You'll show; Of joy You hold great store.

The no - ble and ma - jes - tic ones, Fill me with great de-light
He fills my cup, my lot pre-pares Se- cures to me his grants
My heart with - in me he di- rects To teach me in the night
With my whole be - ing, for my flesh Se - cure - ly finds its rest
Be - fore Your face, at Your right hand, Are plea-suresev- er - more

Psalm 24:1–6

Set to the tune of "Immortal, Invisible, God Only Wise" (*BH*, 1991, #6). Themes: Holiness, Providence

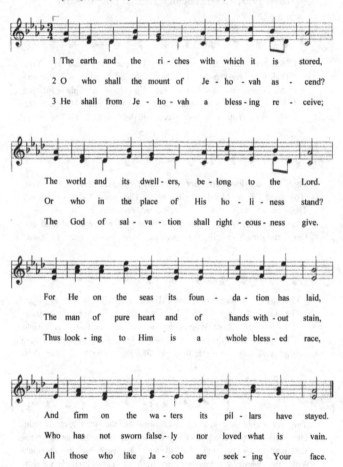

1 The earth and the ri - ches with which it is stored,

2 O who shall the mount of Je - ho - vah as - cend?

3 He shall from Je - ho - vah a bless - ing re - ceive;

The world and its dwell - ers, be - long to the Lord.

Or who in the place of His ho - li - ness stand?

The God of sal - va - tion shall right - eous - ness give.

For He on the seas its foun - da - tion has laid,

The man of pure heart and of hands with - out stain,

Thus look - ing to Him is a whole bless - ed race,

And firm on the wa - ters its pil - lars have stayed.

Who has not sworn false - ly nor loved what is vain.

All those who like Ja - cob are seek - ing Your face.

Psalms Set to Familiar Tunes

Psalm 105:1–4

Set to the tune of "It Came upon a Midnight Clear" (*BH*, 1991, #93). Themes: Evangelism, General Praise

O thank the LORD on his name call. His deeds tell peo - ples all.
O sing to him sing psalms to him, his won - ders all re - call.
Let hearts that seek the LORD re - joice, his ho - ly name a - dore.
O seek Je - ho - vah and his strength, his face seek ev - er - more.

Psalm 128

Set to the tune of "Come, Thou Fount of Every Blessing" (*BH*, 1991, #15). Themes: Parenting, Children, Fatherhood, Fearing the Lord

1 Blessed the man that fears Je - ho - vah and that walk - eth in his ways;
2 Lo, on him that fears Je - ho - vah shall his bless - ed - ness at - tend;
Thou shalt eat of thy hands' la - bor and be pros - pered all thy days.
For Je - ho - vah out of Zi - on shall to thee his bless- ings send.
Like a vine with fruit a - bound - ing in thy house thy wife is found,
Thou shalt see Je - rus' - lem pros - per all thy days till life shall cease;
And like ol - ive plants thy chil - dren com- pass- ing thy ta - ble round.
Thou shalt see thy chil- dren's chil - dren; un - to Is - ra - el be peace.

Psalm 130

Set to the tune of "O for a Thousand Tongues to Sing" (*BH*, 1991, #216). Themes: Waiting on God, Hope

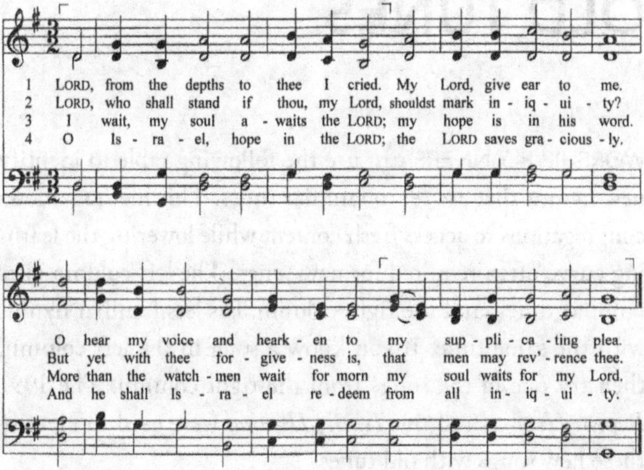
1 LORD, from the depths to thee I cried. My Lord, give ear to me.
2 LORD, who shall stand if thou, my Lord, shouldst mark in - iq - ui - ty?
3 I wait, my soul a - waits the LORD; my hope is in his word.
4 O Is - ra - el, hope in the LORD; the LORD saves gra - cious - ly.
O hear my voice and heark - en to my sup - pli - ca - ting plea.
But yet with thee for - give - ness is, that men may rev' - rence thee.
More than the watch - men wait for morn my soul waits for my Lord.
And he shall Is - ra - el re - deem from all in - iq - ui - ty.

APPENDIX 3

NEW SONGS/ OLD TUNES

WORSHIP PLANNERS can use the following table to identify new hymns that are set to familiar tunes. This method allows congregations to access fresh content while lowering the learning curve often required for new songs. The left column cites familiar tunes, and the right column lists less familiar hymns with the same tune. If you know a song in the left column, then try one of the songs from the right column. The 1991 *Baptist Hymnal* and the *Trinity Hymnal* were used to identify these new songs with old tunes.

Familiar Tune (*Baptist Hymnal*, 1991) *If you know . . .*	**Less Familiar Hymns with the Same Tune . . . *then try . . .***
27: "All Creatures of Our God and King"	*Trinity Hymnal* 289: "A Hymn of Glory Let Us Sing"
43: "This Is My Father's World"	*Baptist Hymnal* 529: "Forever with the Lord"
73: "God Moves in a Mysterious Way"	*Trinity Hymnal* 713: "Great King of Nations, Hear Our Prayer"
77: "Come, Thou, Long Expected Jesus"	*Baptist Hymnal* 36: "Praise the Lord! Ye Heavens Adore Him"

94: "Angels, from the Realms of Glory"	*Trinity Hymnal* 64: "God, the Lord, a King Remaineth"; 286: "Worship Christ, the Risen King!"; 342: "Christ Is Made the Sure Foundation"
126: "All Glory, Laud, and Honor"	*Trinity Hymnal* 75: "O Father, You Are Sovereign"; 156: "O Lord, How Shall I Meet You?"
144: "When I Survey the Wondrous Cross"	*Trinity Hymnal* 427: "Amidst Us Our Beloved Stands"; 485: "O Thou That Hear'st When Sinners Cry"
161: "Crown Him with Many Crowns"	*Trinity Hymnal* 316: "The Mighty God, the Lord"; 575: "Soldiers of Christ, Arise"; 669: "Commit Now All Your Griefs"
197: "Rejoice, the Lord Is King"	*Trinity Hymnal* 18: "You Holy Angels Bright"; 181: "We Come, O Christ, to You"; 301: "Join All the Glorious Names"; 524: "Thy Works, Not Mine, O Christ"
241: "Breathe on Me, Breath of God"	*Baptist Hymnal* 363: "Jesus, Our Lord and King"; *Trinity Hymnal* 516: "Jesus, I Live to Thee"
247: "Come, Thou Almighty King"	*Trinity Hymnal* 447: "Christ for the World We Sing"
277: "Take My Life, and Let It Be Consecrated"	*Trinity Hymnal* 518: "Christ, of All My Hopes the Ground"; 628: "Come, My Soul, Thy Suit Prepare"

297: "Search Me, O God"	*Trinity Hymnal* 388: "Savior, Again to Thy Dear Name We Raise"; 607: "Thy Lovingkindness, Lord, Is Good and Free
306: "Depth of Mercy"	*Trinity Hymnal* 409: "Softly Now the Light of Day"; 694: "Lord, I Lift My Soul to Thee"
339: "Not What My Hands Have Done"	*Trinity Hymnal* 169: "My Heart Does Overflow"; 540: "A Few More Years Shall Roll"; 692: "To You, O Lord, I Fly"
350: "The Church's One Foundation"	*Trinity Hymnal* 311: "Hail to the Lord's Anointed"
379: "Brethren, We Have Met to Worship"	*Baptist Hymnal* 382: "God, the Father of Your People"
388: "Our God Has Made Us One"	*Baptist Hymnal* 30: "Stand Up and Bless the Lord"
414: "O Christ, Our Hope, Our Heart's Desire"	*Trinity Hymnal* 56: "When All Your Mercies, O My God"
481: "Am I a Soldier of the Cross?"	*Baptist Hymnal* 353: "Living Stones"; 358: "This Is the Day the Lord Has Made"; *Trinity Hymnal* 154: "Thou Art the Way"; 458: "What Tho' I Cannot Break My Chain"
493: "Onward, Christian Soldiers"	*Trinity Hymnal* 439: "Christ Shall Have Dominion"
574: "Soldiers of Christ, in Truth Arrayed"	*Trinity Hymnal* 70: "With Glory Clad, with Strength Arrayed"; 337: "O Spirit of the Living God"

587: "Jesus Shall Reign"	*Baptist Hymnal* 13: "From All that Dwell Beneath the Sky"; 70: "How Great Our God's Majestic Name"; *Trinity Hymnal* 16: "Come, Let Us Sing unto the Lord"; 59: "Forever Settled in the Heavens"
604: "Come, All Christians, Be Committed"	*Baptist Hymnal* 377: "Jesus, at Your Holy Table"

APPENDIX 4

CHURCH COVENANT HYMN

The following piece of music is a version of the church covenant used by Auburndale Baptist Church. The tune is an adaptation of an older melody known as "St. Petersburg."

Hav - ing been brought by grace di - vine to
We en gage by the Spi - rit's aid to
We will bring up those in our care, in
We won't for sake the as - sem - bly, nor
Re - pent and be - lieve in Christ and to give
walk in Chri - stian love and strive for know ledge,
the ways of our Lord Je - sus, in love seek-
prayer for our - selves and oth ers. We en gage
up our - selves to Him pro - fess - ing faith through
ho - li - ness, com - fort; to sus - tain the chur -
ing their sal - va - tion. With God's help we will
to watch each oth - er, to aid each oth - er

Church Covenant Hymn

bap - ti - sm, we en - ter in to co - ve-
ch's wor - ship, her or - di - nan - ces, di - sci-
seek to live with care, de - ny - ing world - ly
in suff' - ring, to have kind - ness and sym - path-
nant in the pre - sence of tri - une God most
pline her doc trine; to give cheer - ful - ly in
lusts. We were bur - ied in bap ti - sm and
y, slow in an - ger, quick to for - give. If
Sol - emn - ly and joy - ful - ly with
Sup - port of her min - is - try, the
Raised from the sym - bo - lic grave; we
we move a way, we will soon u-
each oth - er as one bo - dy.
poor's re - lief and gos - pel's spread.
must now lead a ho - ly life.
nite with a gos - pel true church.

NOTES

1. Mark Dever and Paul Alexander, *The Deliberate Church: Building Your Ministry on the Gospel* (Wheaton, IL: Crossway, 2005), 77–88; J. Ligon Duncan III, "Does God Care How We Worship" and "Foundations for Biblically Directed Worship," in *Give Praise to God: A Vision for Reforming Worship*, ed. Phillip Graham Ryken, Derek D. H. Thomas, and J. Ligon Duncan III (Phillipsburg, NJ: P&R, 2003), 17–73. A few other worship elements are sometimes added to this list. The collection of an offering, for instance, has some biblical warrant. The New Testament includes several incidences of churches gathering funds (Acts 4:32–37; 2 Corinthians 9; Philippians 4:14–20). One of Paul's commands situates this offering on "the first day of the week," which coincides with the worship gathering day indicated in the book of Acts (Acts 20:7). Another example, found in Ligon Duncan's essays in *Give Praise to God*, is the practice of vows. We are focusing on the fivefold formulation of preaching, praying, reading, singing, and the ordinances because proponents of the regulative principle share a general consensus on the inclusion of these five elements.
2. Terry Johnson, "Restoring Psalm Singing to Our Worship," in *Give Praise to God*, 257–86.
3. "To Live Is Christ," lyrics by Bob Kauflin and Mark Altrogge. Copyright © 2011 by Sovereign Grace Praise (BMI) (adm. at Capitol CMGPublishing.com) All rights reserved. Used by permission.
4. Dever and Alexander, *The Deliberate Church*; Ryken, Thomas, and Duncan III, eds., *Give Praise to God.*
5. John Foxe, *Fox's Book of Martyrs*, chapter 21; available at www.ccel.org/f/foxe/martyrs/fox121.htm (accessed June 2, 2014).
6. Johnson, "Restoring Psalm Singing to Our Worship," in *Give Praise to God*, 257–86.
7. John Calvin, Preface to the *Genevan Psalter*.